DATE DUE

PRINTED IN U.S.A.

HILLSIDE GARDENING

EVALUATING THE SITE, DESIGNING VIEWS, PLANTING SLOPES

WILLIAM LAKE DOUGLAS

Principal Photographer: Derek Fell

A Fireside Book
published by Simon & Schuster, Inc.
New York

A QUARTO BOOK

Copyright © 1987 by Quarto Marketing Ltd.

Simon and Schuster / Fireside Books,
Published by Simon & Schuster, Inc.
Simon & Schuster Building
Rockefeller Center
1230 Avenue of the Americas
New York, New York 10020

SIMON AND SCHUSTER, FIRESIDE and colophons
are registered trademarks of Simon & Schuster, Inc.

Library of Congress Cataloging in Publication Data
available upon request.

ISBN: 0-671-62223-4
0-671-60240-3 Pbk.

HILLSIDE GARDENING: Evaluating the Site, Designing Views, Planting Slopes
was prepared and produced by
Quarto Marketing Ltd.
15 West 26th Street
New York, New York 10010

Editor: Mary Forsell
Art Director: Mary Moriarty
Photo Editor: Susan M. Duane
Production Manager: Karen L. Greenberg

Typeset By BPE Graphics, Inc.
Color separations by Hong Kong Scanner Craft Company Ltd.
Printed and bound in Hong Kong by Leefung-Asco Printers Ltd.

1 2 3 4 5 6 7 8 9 10
1 2 3 4 5 6 7 8 9 10 Pbk.

DEDICATION

To H and J, whose hillside garden has been both an
inspiration and a resource.

C O N T E N T S

CONTENTS

INTRODUCTION

*T*he hillside garden is a special garden: a challenge for a gardener's technical skills as well as an opportunity to let your imagination soar. In addition to considering and working with such factors as plant shapes, colors, combinations, specialized requirements, and growing characteristics, the hillside gardener must manage technical variables: slope protection, sun angles, and wind direction all play a vital role in the hillside garden.

These ecological constraints are of primary importance in the initial planning stages of a hillside garden. Therefore, you must first consider how you will handle these constraints. An understanding of the environmental opportunities a hillside offers is necessary to the garden's prosperity.

Historical gardens and the work of contemporary landscape architects are instructive examples that will also give you inspiration. Assessing the technical considerations of your own garden and studying how others—past and present—have addressed the problems of a hillside garden will give you a better understanding of the challenges and opportunities that lie ahead.

The investigation of historical references to hillside gardens leads us into every region of the world and through every period of the history of garden design. References are found in surviving gardens as well as in legends, paintings, and local traditions that have passed from one generation to the next. By thoroughly investigating these sources, we can begin to appreciate the complexities and special qualities of a hillside garden and to recognize clues from other gardens that are appropriate for contemporary situations.

It will be instructive, as well, to broaden the definition of "hillside garden" to include anything having a change of elevation—either real or illusory. By observing how these level changes were handled in other gardens, you can learn how problems have been solved, how particular situations have been addressed, and how spectacular effects have been created.

There are many examples illustrating the importance of elevated hill sites in ancient civilization. Mounds were commonly constructed for ceremonial and burial purposes in ancient civilizations and therefore constitute some of the earliest examples of man's interaction with the environment and manipulation of the landscape. Surviving examples of the mounds exist in Asia, Europe, and North America. Pyramids and ziggurats, the most elaborate forms of man-made hills, were built by ancient Egyptians and Sumerians in the Middle East and by the Mayan and Aztec Indians in Central America.

One of the most spectacular uses of a hillside site is the city of Macchu Picchu. Built high in the Peruvian Andes by the Inca civilization, it is at the citadel of mountains that drop almost straight down some two thousand feet to the Urubamba River. It is a city of steps and platforms, carefully constructed of locally quarried stones. Terraces were carved in the hillside for agricultural purposes and were irrigated by water channels that made use of all water falling on the site.

Macchu Picchu is an ancient, classic model for the productive and dramatic use of hillsides.

In ancient Greece, the rocky and often steep terrain influenced the siting of buildings much in the same way that this city on Santorin Island is integrated into its surroundings.

Perhaps the most celebrated example of an elevated garden prior to the Italian Renaissance is the Hanging Gardens of Babylon, built by King Nebuchadnezzar around 600 B.C. Although no remains have ever been found, the garden's design was probably the combination of an agricultural method (growing plants and trees on a terraced hillside) and an architectural monument (the ziggurat itself). Composed of diminishing terraces built on a large platform, the ziggurat was a symbolic connection between heaven and earth. It is thought that waterproofed planting beds in the terraces were supported by arches that held irrigation systems, and hollow brick columns were filled with soil and planted with trees. Similar in concept and construction is the Sumerian Ziggurat at Ur, dating from about 2250 B.C. According to a reconstruction, this monument was about seventy feet high, constructed on a ten-foot terrace above the city. Succeedingly smaller terraces probably were planted with trees, as in the Hanging Gardens, giving the appearance of a tree-covered mountain.

The Dodoni theater in Greece commands a panoramic view. Situated in a narrow valley, its concave form echoes the shape of the depression in the distant hills.

There are indications that the terrace walls were painted black, red, blue, and gold, representing the underworld, the earth, the sky, and the sun.

In Greece, the rocky and irregular terrain influenced the siting of ancient structures; buildings became an integral part of the environment. There was a relationship, as well, between the function of a building and the landscape around it because natural features of sites were linked to architectural function. The bowl-like form of the Dodoni Theater, for instance, echoes the shape of its location and uses the panoramic view of surrounding hills as a backdrop for the theater's stage. The Temple of Athena, on a promontory overlooking the Aegean Sea, also combines function and site. From studying these examples, we learn the importance of evaluating a site and making advantageous use of major features, such as panoramic views and the shape of the terrain as well as relating the site's function to an environmental feature.

Oriental traditions of garden design indicate both an understanding of and an appreciation for hillside sites. Western Europe first became acquainted with Chinese gardens through the travels of Marco Polo (1295); subsequent Western visitors were impressed with the gardens' scale, organization, and composition. Nature was always represented and references to mountains, plants, and water were always included. Significant in Chinese gardens and in Chinese paintings, which afford landscape representations unequaled in any other culture, is the fact that man never dominates; he is only a component—"one of ten thousand"—equal with other parts.

Garden-making in China required not only an appreciation of nature but also the eye of an artist and the imagination of a poet. The collaboration of these three disciplines forms the basis for artistic traditions that have lasted for centuries. Chinese gardens offer opportunities to observe simple events in nature. They are planned for every mood, occasion, and climatic condition, and have been used for centuries as places for environmental observation, poetic contemplation, and meditation.

Japanese gardens emphasize symbolic association. With limited space, Japanese garden makers developed a system whereby every component had a larger, symbolic meaning. Unlike Chinese gardens, which were considered parts of a larger composition, Japanese gardens are meant to be microcosms of everything in nature: mountain ranges, forests, oceans, and so forth. Therefore one rock, carefully selected and positioned in a garden, is appreciated both for its own unique characteristics as well as for its representation of a mountain range or a hill. It is this symbolism that adds a layer of complexity to garden design in Japan and offers an opportunity for garden makers everywhere to learn by example and expand their garden horizons. The premise of attaching metaphorical significance to ordinary elements can serve as a provocative point of departure when planning any garden.

In Japanese-style gardens such as this one near Philadelphia, the individual components allude to larger schemes of nature: A plant may represent a forest, or a rock may signify a mountain range.

Perhaps the most spectacular example of hillside gardening occurs in the Italian Renaissance. The growth of commercial centers around Venice, Florence, and Genoa led to the establishment of a wealthy merchant class for whom villas in the countryside were a necessity. It is in these villas (the term applies to the buildings as well as to the landscape settings) that we can see the primary contribution of the Renaissance to garden design: the system of spatial organization, the richness of design details, and the unity of design elements within the entire composition.

For the most part the landscape of Italy is hilly; therefore sites for villas were often on the tops or sides of steep hills. Making these sites useful meant terracing the hillside, often resulting in engineering feats previously unknown. The terraces produced were frequently small and contained rooms arranged in an ordered progression. Decorative ramps and ceremonial staircases were often used to connect the spaces. With loggias and windows, buildings opened onto the garden to take advantage of views into the surrounding countryside. Thus the view became an important consideration in the design of the garden. In addition to providing views, hillside sites provided the necessary changes of elevation that allowed for widespread use of elaborate fountains and water features. Hillside streams were manipulated to create complicated fountains run by natural water pressure. These fountains were designed to make musical sounds, operate animated figures, gush in a variety of effects from single spurts to multiple sprays, and, to the delight of Renaissance hosts, shower unsuspecting guests from unusual sources.

From these gardens we can gain an understanding of how wonderful a hillside garden can be. Careful observation of how these gardens were designed will serve as inspiration for your own garden's design as well as supply details for design and construction.

Vertical interest at Versailles—as well as in other French gardens of seventeenth-century France—is provided by architectural and horticultural elements. Horizontal patterns, designed to be viewed from above, enliven the ground plane.

Just as gardens in the Italian Renaissance offer lessons in how to treat a hillside site, gardens of seventeenth-century France offer ideas on how to handle relatively flat situations, exaggerating effects to create the illusion of a change in elevation where none, or only a slight difference, exists. France, unlike Italy, is generally flat; yet seventeenth-century garden designers, anxious to replicate the popular Italian styles of the period, used large ramps, grand staircases, and repetition of forms (plants as well as statues) to make gradual changes of elevation seem more important. Long basins or reflecting pools were excavated, with the dual effect of creating features lower than their surroundings as well as offering opportunities for vertical elements, like sculptures or fountains. (Because of the slight change of elevation, however, the fountains were not always successful.)

It has been rather convincingly documented that Andre Le Nôtre, the primary garden designer of the period and the architect of gardens at both Vaux-le-Vicomte and Versailles, used the science of optics to make features seem larger or smaller, closer or farther away in the landscape. By using these optical illusions, he was able to exaggerate even more the slight changes of elevation the terrain offered, creating effects that recalled the spirit, if not the substance, of his Italian predecessors.

All of these techniques, subtle as they are, contributed to a style that retains the essence of the hillside garden's splendor and extravagance. Depending on how faithfully they are adapted, these motifs can make flat sites more interesting and impart authority and grandeur to a hillside site.

From eighteenth- and nineteenth-century England, the next stops on this garden-history odyssey, we learn of the significance of composed views in the landscape, and how combinations of plant material with different forms, colors, and textures create a feeling of height and a sense of elevation change. In all the arts, allegorical references to ancient mythology frequently occur during the eighteenth century. Architects built structures based on classical proportions and garden makers created scenes that resembled the paintings of Salvator Rosa, Claude Lorrain, and Nicolas Poussin. These paintings frequently included classically inspired temples or objects—often in ruins—on hills or on prominent locations in the untamed wilderness. The gardens inspired by the paintings included structures called "eyecatchers," objects that were visible only at selected and predetermined locations in the landscape. They were meant to evoke a specific emotion in the viewer,

Le Notre's garden at Vaux-le-Vicomte is a relatively flat site. Optical illusions, long ramps, and vertical elements add complexity and interest to the garden.

These garden steps lead the visitor through colorful plantings of annuals and perennials that have different textures and forms.

and often were employed for no purpose other than as a visual reference. By limiting and controlling the observer's view in these gardens, the designer could carefully compose both the view as well as the progression of the observer in the space. Although this "management" of activity

and views should be remembered when designing any garden, a hillside site, because of its inherent change in elevation, offers the designer excellent opportunities to take advantage of these techniques.

With the fascination of Victorian England for

horticulture came the practice of creating landscape compositions of as many varieties of plant forms, colors, and textures as possible. Besides providing visual interest (or, as some might say today, confusion), this practice shows what effects can be produced by using mounded plant forms with vertical shapes and by employing different layers of plant forms to create a feeling of depth, space, and change of elevation.

In America, hills have had great significance in the design of the built environment. Traditionally, hilltops have been favored locations for community-oriented buildings such as schools, churches, museums, public facilities, and civic buildings because of the view to the hill's top from below and the fact that panoramic views of the surrounding community are possible. Called "prospect," this phenomenon illustrates an important consideration when evaluating hillside sites. What are the views *from* the hillside? What are the views *to* the hillside? The significance of the answers to

Gardens typical of the California School, such as this one in Carmel designed by Thomas Church, feature informal plantings and rooms for outdoor living.

these questions depends on the particular site's function and the relationship of the hillside site to its immediate surroundings. Considered during the planning stages before anything is actually built, these questions will often dictate the organization of the site as well as the location of proposed features on the site.

In America, the mid-twentieth century saw the development of what is now called the "California School" of landscape design. It was a reaction against the formality of earlier landscape-design traditions and a design response based on the considerations of site and climate. Landscape architects, particularly James Rose, Thomas Church, and Garrett Eckbo, designed residential gardens (often on sites of less than one acre) for clients who were interested in using outdoor spaces for daily activities and maintaining them without paid assistance. There was little separation between inside and outside spaces—one merged with the other, creating continuous rooms for living. The designers made extensive use of decks and terraces for outdoor living and paid careful attention to small details. Many of these gardens were created in California first because Church, Eckbo, and their colleagues were practicing there. Soon, however, the philosophy of the California School spread across the country and designs of this type were featured in popular publications of the time. This development—unique to America—certainly ranks as one of the most significant events in the history of garden design and has direct implications on our study of hillside gardens.

This brief look at hillside gardens in garden history offers important clues to garden-making. Historical landmarks can serve as inspirations for the design of your hillside garden. Keep in mind, however, that consideration of components of these gardens should be influenced by your garden's functions and site and your own personal design preferences.

CHAPTER ONE

ENVIRONMENTAL CONSIDERATIONS

As with other sites, planning a hillside garden requires a comprehensive environmental evaluation. In this initial stage of garden-making, it would be advantageous to consult a landscape architect. Trained in being able to "read" a site in terms of its physical characteristics and limitations, a landscape architect can make suggestions that will save time, effort, and expenditure down the road.

In fact, the participation of a landscape architect would be beneficial in all stages of hillside garden design, from site selection to final design and plant selection. And hiring a landscape architect does not mean that you relinquish the opportunity to make personal design decisions. Most landscape architects welcome the participation of a client in all stages of development and are willing to let the owner retain responsibility for as many decisions as desired.

Collaborating with a landscape architect will be much easier if you have a general understanding of relevant environmental factors that have an impact on your site. The geological characteristics of a hill as well as its orientation toward sun angles and prevailing winds are important initial considerations. Individually and collectively, these will play a major role in the prosperity of plants in the garden. By designing with these environmental considerations in mind, the location of features is easily determined and the success of your garden is all but guaranteed.

All: *Often the best plants for a garden are those that are native to the site. They appear naturally as a response to the site's soil, water, wind, and solar conditions and are usually self-generating.*

SOIL

*H*aving a general knowledge of your garden site's soil is essential in making decisions about what plants and structures the site will support. Soil is composed of several ingredients: solid particles of sand, clay and rocks, decaying vegetative matter, living organisms, water, and air. The soil's texture is determined by the consistency of its components and by the presence or absence of organic matter in it. It is the balance of these elements that will determine the fertility of the soil as well as the type of growth it will support.

Left: *At the Berkeley Botanical Garden in California, rocky, arid conditions support cactus and related succulents.* **Above:** *The Leonard Bush Rock Garden in New Jersey is an ideal site for phlox, ferns, and dogwood because it is moist yet well drained.*

The characteristics of soil can be altered relatively easily by the addition of sand, humus (decayed vegetative matter), or by chemical fertilizers. A heavy soil will tend to retain water and should be broken up by the addition of sand to facilitate drainage. The capacity of a loose, sandy soil to retain moisture can be improved by the addition of humus, peat, or decayed leaves. Minerals—primarily nitrogen, phosphorus, and potassium—are added to the soil through commercially available fertilizers with proportions appropriate to the desired result.

The acidity or alkalinity of a soil determines what can be grown in it. This rating is measured in pH degrees, from 0 to 14, with a low number (pH 4, for instance) being more acid, and a high number (pH 8) being more alkaline. The best soil for growing most plants has a pH measurement of about 6 to 6.5.

Vegetative, mineral, and chemical nutrients are easily added to soil to alter its natural composition, and periodic replacement of these elements is essential for a productive garden.

Determining the condition of your soil is a relatively simple procedure. Most garden centers and nurseries sell soil-test kits that are reliable and easy to use. Another suggestion is to consult with the county or provincial agricultural-extension agent. In most areas, this service is provided at no cost. Other effective early steps are to notice what grows on the site and to consult neighbors and nearby gardeners for advice. What grows naturally is a quick clue to the kind of soil and water conditions present. Remember that a range of plants can grow on each soil type. Keep in mind, too, that it is far easier to use native plants ("native" to the site as well as "native" to the region) for a garden than to try to radically alter the composition of soil to support a plant that is inappropriate to the soil. For those "must-have" plants that require conditions different from those present, consider using pots or containers that can easily (and inexpensively) be filled with the special soil mixtures these plants require.

pH Chart

pH 3	very acid sand
pH 4	very acid peat
pH 4.4	very acid loams and heavy soils
pH 4.7	organic material not affected by bacteria is located below
pH 5.1	phosphates almost unavailable below this point
pH 6.5	ideal for most soils
pH 7.0	neutral
pH 7.5	deficiencies in trace elements in most plants in soil above this pH
pH 8	chalky soil

Rough Test for Soil Quality

SOIL SURFACE	CHARACTER
Clay	stiff and plastic; can be worked with hands into shapes
Clay loam	sticky; can be "shined" by rubbing a little with hands
Medium loam	neither stiff and plastic nor gritty
Sand	gritty; will not stick to hands
Sandy loam	gritty; some will stick to fingers
Silty loam	feels silky or soapy in hands

Rhododendrons thrive on a cool mountain site where there is plenty of moisture in the air, and the sunlight is filtered through the trees.

SUN

Solar orientation is an important consideration for the hillside garden both when selecting plants as well as when making decisions about locations of structural features. The ideal exposure from a solar point of view is southern to southwestern, because of the lengthy sun exposure during summer months. The least desirable exposure for gardens is northern.

Not all hillside sites are blessed with ideal conditions, however. What can you do to mitigate the adverse effects of too much or too little sun? Place terraces or planting beds for vegetables in locations that will take maximum advantage of the sun. If there is too much sun, plant evergreen or deciduous trees to provide shade for plants or outdoor activities. Structures such as pergolas, gazebos, or lanais can be built and covered with roofs, vines, or fabric such as canvas or shade cloth.

When more sun is desired for plants, consider constructing south walls to reflect light and heat. If there is too little sun getting through because of tree growth, eliminate some trees or prune branches to allow more light into the space. With too little light available, you may be deprived of the dramatic effects created by light and shadow. Sunlight streaming directly to the ground and through foliage creates intricate and ever-changing patterns and provides a constant shift in the appearance of colors in the garden. Influenced by qualities of light, colors of garden plants will reflect the interplay of sunlight and shadow. Color is an important design element in the garden, and it plays a part in spatial perception: Cool, light colors visually enlarge a garden space while warm, dark colors make a garden seem smaller and more confined. Gardens with flowers of a pale color—particularly white—will appear larger than a garden of the same size with multicolored flowers.

While the orientation of your garden cannot be changed, it can be advantageously exploited by using plants appro-

This sunny hillside is equipped with a stairway so that visitors can walk among the colorful mass plantings of fall-blooming chrysanthemums.

Often the wildflowers that exist naturally on a site are all that is needed for a spectacular hillside garden.

Siting a home on the southern slope of a hillside provides many benefits. The wooded crest of the hill shields the house from northerly winds, and the southern exposure allows a profusion of wildflowers to grow nearby.

Overlooking the Mediterranean, this garden on the Côte d'Azur takes advantage of the southern exposure. Terraces scale the hillside, and the pools of water reflect the forms and colors of plants and the hues of the sky.

Microclimates

All regions have microclimates, that is, small areas within each hardiness zone that vary widely from the general climate. Microclimates can be the result of a number of factors: land slopes, bodies of water, or wind currents. The temperature within a microclimate may be ten to twenty degrees warmer or colder than its surroundings. Similarly, the growing season for plants may be weeks longer or shorter than it is a few miles away.

How microclimates affect your hillside environment depends largely on how you site your garden. Among the things to be considered are shade, exposure to sun and wind, and possible frost pockets.

Often, the use of shelterbelts is the first step taken to create favorable microclimate. In upland or coastal areas the wind shelter provided by tree belts can influence the temperature of the leeward (downwind) areas. The worth of such shelter will depend on wind strength and ground form. Shelterbelts of somewhat open form are often found to be more effective than dense belts, since dense growths will likely cause wind turbulence on the leeward side. A way of combating this effect is to create a gradual lifting effect on the wind by placing low shrubs starting on rising ground and following these low-growing forms with increasingly taller plants and trees.

Warm air separates rapidly, especially at night when it isn't as windy. As a result, the warm air rises, and cold air settles into valleys. Microclimates are created in hilly regions where hilltop and valley residents can experience a significant difference in temperature.

Hilltops are not considered ideal places to garden because of the susceptibility of these sites to high winds and storms. Use the top of a hill as a buffer for a garden planted just below. A location partway up a sunny hillside is an excellent site for a garden, particularly if the hill slopes south or southeast. Protected from the wind, this garden will have a beneficial solar orientation and will be where air can descend to the valley below.

Hillside Gardens and Microclimate

1. Cold air settles into valley and creates frost pockets.
2. Shrub windbreaks protect garden from cold air.
3. Full sun greets this well-drained area.
4. Chilly, windy hilltop where trees buffer gardens below.
5. Very little sunlight shines directly on windy northwestern slope.

As a result of careful planning, this patio is situated where it can have areas of sun and shade. Banked planters buffer prevailing winds.

priate to the solar conditions. Again, look around at adjacent property for clues to what grows well and looks attractive in particular situations. South-facing slopes are well suited to plants with brightly colored flowers. Northern slopes, by contrast, may be planted in dark or pastel colors to let shadows play on the subtle shadings of less showy plants.

When locating patios in relation to sun, remember that south or west is the best orientation for these structures in temperate climate zones. For very hot climates, however, patios are better located with a northern orientation, taking advantage of the shade. An eastern-located patio is also appropriate , since strong morning sun will taper off toward afternoon.

*An evergreen hedge of hemlock—*Tsuga canadensis—*can buffer unwanted winds and screen undesirable views.*

WIND

*K*nowing the direction of prevailing winds is another important consideration. Warming winds, generally from the south and west, are beneficial and should be taken advantage of, whereas winds from the north tend to be cold and harsh and should be screened or deflected. Structural baffles (such as fences, walls, and buildings) and plant materials (particularly broadleaf evergreens) can provide windbreaks that will deflect undesirable winds or channel beneficial air currents into a particular part of a larger area.

On windy sites plants need to obtain a good roothold early in their development. For this reason, it is preferable to choose young, sturdy material for windy situations. Take care especially when planting evergreens and conifers, which, if planted when they are too mature, may topple easily. In general, most trees and other material will need staking; small bushy plants should be planted so that they lean away from prevailing winds.

In making decisions about site conditions, don't forget to consider views as a design determinant. It is ideal when the screening of an unattractive view coincides with the deflection of an undesirable wind current, or when the opening of a view to the south allows warming winds into the garden. But when this does not happen, be prepared to take appropriate action based on your priorities. A spectacular view may—or may not—be worth the price of prevailing winds from the north. Experiment with solutions that combine structural elements with plant material: Perhaps part of a view can be framed by a fence or a hedge that will enhance the view while deflecting most of the undesirable winds.

This evergreen windbreak of white pine—Pinus strobus—had to be planted when the specimen was quite young so it could obtain a good roothold.

NATURAL GROWTHS

Mass plantings of azaleas, pinks, yellow baskets, tulips, and daffodils are an effective means of protecting a hillside from erosion.

When considering and evaluating the natural components of the site, pay special attention to what is growing there in its undeveloped state. With an unfamiliar site, it may be advisable to experience at least one complete growing cycle before making any alterations, allowing seasonal plants, such as spring bulbs and summer wildflowers, the opportunity to make their presence known. The plants that are already on the site are there for an important reason: They have succeeded in tolerating the specific conditions of the site. Do not hastily dispose of any plants, particularly those that some people would initially consider to be weeds. What grows in a particular area may be the only thing that will grow there without totally changing soil characteristics or subsoil conditions, both of which can be prohibitively expensive operations. And even if a plant appears to be a weed, it will most likely have more than one redeeming quality—an ability to survive difficult site conditions, a summer blooming period, an interesting seedpod, or a brightly colored spring growth. What exists on the site in its undeveloped state should also give the gardener an indication of what kind of garden can be developed. One cannot expect to change an open site to a woodland in less than twenty or thirty years. Nor should one expect a wooded site to suddenly be filled with summer wildflowers if it is denuded of its established stand of trees. Radical changes are environmentally disastrous, and, depending on the severity of the changes that follow the removal of established vegetation, the site may never recover.

Starting with what is there provides years of established growth for the gardener to work with, particularly when there are trees on the site. While conserving existing vegetation, however, the gardener's individual needs—to open a view or bring in the sun, for example—may necessitate removal of some of what exists. Carefully consider what the long-term effects will be, since it takes thirty or forty years to replace a well-developed tree taken out in a matter of hours!

By allowing native wildflowers to grow freely, a pleasingly natural effect is created.

Native wildflowers have an ability to survive difficult site conditions while also providing attractive garden highlights.

Shade-loving ground covers, such as the ice plant shown here, are ideal for planting under trees.

STEPS TO SITE ANALYSIS

All of these considerations are part of what the landscape architect calls the "site analysis." The information compiled here is vital to the subsequent decision-making process of determining where specific features will go. A site analysis can be simple (looking only at a few topics) or complicated (requiring a series of overlays, tables, and diagrams). The more detailed your site analysis, the more useful the information will be later on in the design process. For most residential sites, all pertinent site information—including sun angles, existing vegetation and site features, views to save or screen, and points of access—can be shown on one scale drawing, using lines, arrows, bubbles, and other graphic symbols. You can compile some of this information yourself; the more technical data should be collected and evaluated by a landscape architect. Although this drawing may look like the scribblings of a child it will become the basis for your site's design. In general, the following elements should be included in a site analysis:

1. Property outline, with appropriate measurements drawn to scale. Denote the direction north with an arrow and provide an indication of the scale (such as 1" = 10' = 0").

2. Location of any existing buildings or site features, both natural and man-made (fences, rock outcroppings, foundations, steps, etc.).

3. Locations of existing utilities: sewerage (storm and sani-

Recognizing what exists naturally on a site is a major step toward understanding what kind of garden your site can support.

This garden takes optimal advantage of the mountains in the background.

Natural rock outcrops and existing vegetation—in this case, yellow lady's slipper (Cypripedium calceolus)—are some of the elements that should be included in a site analysis.

tary), electrical lines, telephone, etc.

4. Location and configuration of bodies of water (streams, bogs, etc.).

5. Location and outlines of existing vegetation, including size and condition of major trees and shrubs. Note any unusually attractive—or unattractive—plant features.

6. General outline of contours, showing any abrupt changes of slope and elevation. Show elevation at entries to structures and at the top and bottom of steps, walls, etc.

7. Existing circulation patterns (roads, walks, paths, etc.). Show connections with other features on site, as well as direction to features off site.

8. Wind patterns, sun angles, and any other climatic feature that may have an effect on the design.

9. Locations of major views or scenic features indicated by stars or asterisks. Arrows will indicate where the best points of observation are, and the direction of the best views.

10. Areas that should not be disturbed for various reasons (wildlife nesting area, difficult terrain, etc.).

11. Areas that should be preserved or should be developed with only a minimum of features.

Finally, don't hesitate to make any notations you feel necessary to describe the conditions of your site. The site analysis is a diagrammatic record of what is there as well as a summary of information that will be used later on in the development of a design. Remember that the information gathered and recorded here will determine the final design. It is far better to have too much information at this initial stage than too little!

CHAPTER TWO

ROOMS WITH A VIEW

A room with a view, and you,
With no one to worry us,
No one to hurry us—through
This dream we've found.
    —"A Room With a View" from
        This Year of Grace

When Noël Coward wrote of a room with a view, he probably had an urban situation in mind; however, if the gardener considers the hillside as an opportunity for a series of rooms with a view, the hillside garden takes on new dimensions.

By virtue of its location, the hillside garden suggests a view beyond the garden itself. Fortunate are those whose hillsides overlook a bucolic landscape or the sprawling development of a city below. In either case—whether the view is urban or rural—there are probably features that you would like to emphasize and other aspects of the views you would rather not look at every day. Using either man-made structures or plants, views can be emphasized, embellished, or eliminated altogether.

A view of an urban area incorporated into an outdoor design scheme, such as this one in San Francisco, can contribute immeasurably to the success of a garden.

VIEWS FROM ABOVE

The garden makers of the Italian Renaissance developed the idea of the hillside garden as a series of outdoor rooms, joined to one another by steps or ramps. Often, these rooms were meant to be viewed from above as a pattern on the ground plane or in combination with the panorama of the adjacent countryside. Water parterres, topiary, and hedges clipped into elaborate mazes were common features in these small, contained rooms. Frequently, towers or other structures were added to facilitate observation of what was below.

The French, however, elaborated on the theme of appreciating gardens from above, making extensive use of intricate patterns knowns as *parterres de broderie*. These spaces replicated delicate, lacelike designs with low, clipped hedges and beds of colored gravel or crushed stone. These gardens, meant to be observed from above, were built below the main reception rooms of a residence or below a balustraded terrace. Patterns were geometric as well as figural, sometimes simple but often complex.

From the seventeenth to the nineteenth century, this idea appears periodically in English gardens as well, showing particular strength during the early 1600s and the late 1800s. As interest in naturalized landscapes grew during the eighteenth and nineteenth centuries, interest in parterre gardens waned, only to reappear in the late-Victorian period. A revival of interest in parterre gardens in both public parks and private country houses, together with an almost maniacal fascination with exotic and colorful plants, made these parterres lively and entertaining. This technique was known as "carpet bedding," because low-growing plants were planted closely together to resemble the intricate patterns and color combinations of Oriental carpets. We may not have the physical ex-

To play up a beautiful view, such as this one in San Simeon, California, frame the scene with vertical elements and keep the foreground simple so that attention is directed to the view.

An elegant water parterre in Palm Grove, Bermuda, is a variation on the classic French parterre garden.

panse of a French garden to work with, and we may not share the flower-mania of the Victorians, or be able to employ the staff of gardeners required for these elaborate garden designs; nevertheless, we should appreciate the lessons these gardens offer about the visual impact of viewing a garden from above.

Even if it is only by ten or fifteen feet, viewing a garden from above is completely different from experiencing it at ground level by walking through it. Too often, only the latter is considered in planning, thereby eliminating the opportunity to appreciate a garden in plain view. Recognizing this, a garden designer may add an observation platform at the top of the hillside, where viewers can sit and enjoy the view out as well as the garden below. Another idea is to include a clipped hedge in your garden in the form of a maze or a pattern that becomes apparent only from a height. It is surprises like these that add a special quality to a hillside garden.

Above and below: *Knot gardens, such as these that incorporate herbs, make the most visual impact when viewed from above. Gravel can be added for textural diversity and color contrast. Herbs are particularly appropriate for knot gardens.*

VIEWS FROM BELOW

Gardens can also be designed to be experienced from lower levels looking up. This is particularly applicable for gardens in front of older residences above street level. There is frequently a change of ten to twenty feet between the street and the structure in such situations, and the structure is already prominent because of its raised elevation. It is important that the visitor's movement to the house corresponds to the importance lent by the raised elevation of the house. In the visual sequence from street level to front door, offer the visitor a variety of experiences. Pay careful attention to the combinations of hard surfaces (steps, walls, etc.), the variety and combinations of plants, and the route of access. While a straight line is the most direct route from point A (the street) to point B (the front door), practical, short routes are not always the most interesting way of moving through a garden. Changes of scene—in the form of garden sculpture, interesting trees, or compelling

An unusual bank of mosses is a serene foreground for the structure beyond.

The view from this lower grassy area to the curving stone staircase and woodland beyond provides intrigue and prompts the visitor to explore other levels of the garden.

The paths and plantings in this Kyoto, Japan, garden direct attention up the hillside.

In the Vaux-le-Vicomte garden in France, repetition of forms guides the eye up the ramps and into other areas.

The shape of the stairway is echoed by the hedges flanking it.

views—add excitement to the journey to the front door. The design technique known as *sequence* is reflected in this approach to landscape design. By taking visitors on a circuitous route, a sense of excitement, expectation, and mystery increases the enjoyment of the garden and allows the different features of the garden to be seen.

By allowing the access from one area to another to be indirect, focal points (textures, plants, and sculpture) can be established along the way that will make the distance seem physically shorter and visually more interesting.

With an indirect system of circulation through a hillside garden, retaining walls may be necessary. Besides their obvious function, retaining walls offer an opportunity to focus eye-level attention on focal points or specimen plants. Beds can be created below the walls; flowers can be planted in pots on top of the wall; and planting pockets for vines or alpines can be left in the wall.

BORROWED VIEWS

The borrowed view is a familiar technique in Japanese gardens.

From the Japanese comes the concept of "borrowed scenery." Traditionally small and self-contained, Japanese gardens are enlarged by making visual use of features on adjacent property. While not physically a part of the garden, the presence of these features—a stand of trees, a view, a structure—contributes to the garden by being included in its design. This is an easy and economical way to add interest to your garden. Frame a view with hedges or tall trees, and it will become a special feature and a part of your garden, although it may belong to your neighbors.

A word of caution: When visually bringing a distant view or feature into the design of your garden, make a decision about what will dominate in the garden's design—the foreground (the garden itself), or the background (the view or feature). Competition between the two will destroy the effectiveness of each one. Emphasize the foreground by limiting the views outside of it and by adding color, texture, and detail to the garden. Conversely, making the foreground simple will allow the view beyond to dominate.

NIGHTTIME VIEWS

*I*f your hillside overlooks a city, don't forget to consider how a fence or hedge can affect a nocturnal scene. A spectacular nighttime view is reason enough to design an area in your garden just for the pleasure of looking. If the daytime view is not all that attractive, one rule to follow is to avoid installing a complicated planting in the foreground that will compete with a spectacular view in the background. One or the other should dominate; emphasizing both will destroy the effectiveness and special character of each.

Constructing a mock-up of the structure you propose will be helpful in judging its effects at various times during the day. In fact, full-sized mock-ups, constructed of inexpensive materials, are sometimes used by landscape architects as an effective way of providing the client with a realistic impression of a proposed wall or fence. While this may seem an extravagant or unnecessary expense, it is a possibility worth careful consideration, particularly if the fence or wall will be a major feature of the garden, or if the view screened or emphasized is of major importance in the garden's design.

Finally, by thinking of your hillside garden as a room, or as a series of rooms, you will be able to address larger issues that will affect the details of the design: What impact will views have? What times of day are the most visually exciting? How can existing features be used? What sequence of movement is appropriate from one area to the next? All of these questions will help you plan your hillside garden and take maximum advantage of the site's potential.

Above and below: *Both of these outdoor spaces make visual use of features that aren't part of the gardens themselves. Water and distant views become attractive components of the visual composition.*

CHAPTER THREE

TECHNICAL ASPECTS

A garden is composed of a variety of elements—plants, man-made features, earth forms, and areas for functional activities. A hillside garden gives the designer an opportunity to use these elements in conjunction with a change in elevation, enabling a variety of effects ranging from the subtle to the dramatic. Changing the land to accommodate the plans you have for your garden requires a certain knowledge of technical consideration.

When making a hillside garden, certain technical aspects must be considered as a necessary part of the design. An understanding of ground forms and how they can be used is essential; skillfulness in manipulating a site's ground plane is the key to a pleasing design and an exciting garden. As with the environmental considerations discussed earlier, technical aspects of garden-making often require the expertise of a professional. If you understand the technical language used in planning an outdoor space, collaboration between you and your landscape architect will be much more productive.

An important feature of Middleton Place, South Carolina—one of North America's oldest gardens—is its terraced hillside that leads to ponds beyond it. Studying these terraces is an instructive method for understanding the concept of contour lines: Each terrace represents one line; the difference in elevation between each terrace is the contour interval.

BASICS OF TOPOGRAPHY

Contour lines are imaginary lines that connect points of equal elevation. They are, theoretically, measured from sea level and are shown on topographic maps as narrow lines with an adjacent number, indicating the distance above sea level or a known reference point. Drawn on surveys, maps, and the site plans of landscape architects, contour lines describe the "lay of the land" as it exists or as it is proposed. (When existing and proposed contours are shown on the same plane, existing contours are indicated as continuous lines, and proposed contours are shown as broken ones.)

Contours that are widely spaced indicate a relatively flat site, or a gently sloping terrain. Closely spaced contours describe a steep situation, where there is a rapid change of elevation. To the trained eye, contour lines describe surface conditions from which other information—primarily drainage characteristics—can be inferred.

The distance between contour lines is known as the *contour interval*. On maps, topographic surveys, or plans, this interval is indicated or can be easily deduced by noting intervals between numbered contours. For large areas, the interval is usually large: ten feet, twenty feet, fifty feet. For smaller sites, the interval is smaller, usually one foot.

Features in the landscape, such as existing trees, tops and bottoms of walls and steps, and floor elevations are described on plans by *spot elevations,* which indicate the elevation of the particular feature at its exact location. For paved surfaces such as terraces and drives, where rapid drainage is necessary, spot elevations are often expressed with decimal equivalents: 28.50, for instance, is 28'6" above a known reference point.

The *slope* of the hillside describes how the ground changes in relation to a level

Above: *A natural slope provides a gardener with a landscaping challenge: to select an interesting palette of plants that will complement the natural contours of the site.* ***Below left:*** *A sharp change in elevation lends drama to a garden.* ***Below right:*** *Such changes in elevation can be created by using retaining walls.*

In this New Jersey garden, a combination of ground covers—including the purple-blooming Ajuga reptans*—and wildflowers drift up the slope.*

plane. It is usually expressed as a percentage and is calculated by dividing the vertical change of elevation between two points by the horizontal distance between them. This is represented by the formula $G = D/L$, where G is the gradient percentage, D is the difference in elevation, and L is the horizontal length between two points. A hilltop is described as a series of circular shapes, with the highest part indicated graphically by the smallest shape (the top is usually indicated by a spot elevation).

When considering drainage, remember that water flows down, perpendicular to the contour. If the slope is gradual—that is, the contours are evenly and widely spaced—the flow will be gradual and will not disturb the planting or soil. If the slope is steep, however, the runoff will be rapid with the potential of causing erosion.

Exposed rock formations and mounded plantings visually enhance the gentle slope of this garden. A device employed here is the use of rounded forms, which can make an incline appear to be steeper.

SLOPE PROTECTION

Native rocks are used in the construction of this retaining wall. Spaces left in the wall provide room for small plants to grow as attractive accents.

*Railroad ties can be used in a variety of interesting ways. **Above:** The railroad ties become steps that blend nicely with their surroundings. **Right:** Another effective usage of ties is as retaining walls, which can also incorporate steps. Whenever possible, use old ties, as new ones are not weathered, which can result in preservatives leaching into adjacent planting areas. **Far right:** A deck extends living space into the treetops and allows for elevated observation of the garden below.*

Changing the natural slope of a site will often require some form of protection from erosion. This can be provided by mechanical, horticultural, or structural methods. Often, a combination of these methods will provide the best protection for large areas (such as sites disturbed by major construction). For smaller sites, usually one method will be adequate. Keep in mind that major structural changes to a slope should be made only with the professional advice of experienced practitioners. Care and sensitivity should be taken when disturbing landforms around buildings and existing plants, since even the slightest alteration may cause permanent damage. A general rule of thumb when altering the ground around an existing tree is to leave the area within the tree's drip line (the area directly beneath of tree's branches) undisturbed. Should construction within the drip line be unavoidable, proceed with caution. Do as much of the work as possible manually, rather than with heavy equipment. Keep in mind that any root destruction or subsurface disturbance will have a corresponding effect on the visible part of the tree. The effect will not be immediate, but it is inevitable and usually irreversible.

Slope Solutions

A change of elevation, particularly if it is dramatic, creates inherent interest and character in any landscape. In sloping and undulating sites, there are more opportunities for the gardener to create interesting plant combinations and visual features than in a flat situation. Slopes can be minor or extreme, and they can be natural or man-made. What a landowner can do with a sloping site depends on subsurface conditions, on how steep the slope is, and what kind of effect is desired.

A shallow slope, for example, can be converted without a great deal of work to a series of level areas or plateaus, connected by steps or ramps. Sometimes, all that is needed is a terrace with angled pathways leading down the slope with a retaining wall at the very bottom. For sites with greater slopes, retaining walls can be used to create different levels, with a system of steps and landings for ease of movement.

All types of hillside slopes can benefit from a deck. Before you start construction, evaluate your family's needs in relationship to the possibilities of the site. Consult with a landscape architect to develop a program for new construction as well as for advice on carrying out plans that are appropriately engineered in terms of safety and other factors.

You might want your deck to mirror the shape of your back-yard, or a room in the house. Remember that a deck can surround mature trees or plants, so professional advice will be helpful in ensuring that new construction does not harm existing material. A deck is an opportunity to link house and hillside, providing spaces for outdoor living and observation of the landscape.

Mechanical Methods

Mechanical protection involves changing the landform to reduce the slope and slow the rate of runoff. This can include cutting a steep slope or filling a low spot to provide a more even grade. For large areas, heavy equipment is necessary. The ground can be sculpted by the installation of slight berms (mounds) or depressions to channel runoff into a desired direction. By channeling water in the direction of existing low spots and by enlarging these low spots to accommodate runoff, you can effectively add a stream system or pond to a garden. If this is not desired, subsurface drainage systems (drain tiles, perforated pipes, or catch basins) can be installed to eliminate runoff. These systems can spread the water out over a larger area, disposing of runoff by natural percolation. If the amount of runoff is large, the system could connect with existing storm sewer lines.

Above: By channeling water in the direction of a slope, a gardener can create a small stream. **Right:** Water flows naturally down the slopes of this hillside and into the drainage system at Nemours. With walls constructed from different-sized rocks and a bed of native stones, this artificially constructed stream integrates easily with the landscape.

Wildflowers and native grasses are an effective means of slope protection for gentle slopes. Aside from a periodic mowing, generally little maintenance is required.

Horticultural Methods

Horticultural methods can be used as a basic form of erosion control for slopes of up to a 10-percent grade. Grasses and wildflowers are particularly appropriate for this purpose, since they will germinate easily and their root systems will hold the topsoil in place until more substantial vegetation can naturally take over. Often wildflowers and grasses are used in conjunction with fabric matting, contour-wattling techniques, or the installation of rooted cuttings.

Fabric matting is designed to stabilize banks and slopes by holding the soil in place while allowing vegetation to become established. Made of woven nylon or natural fibers (coconut fiber, straw, and cotton thread), these blankets are designed for a variety of situations, from steep slopes to drainage ditches. Generally, they are used on large-scale projects, where quick protection of a large area is required.

Critical factors that determine the weight and content of the appropriate fabric include the use of the site, its soil composition, the length and degree of slope, the amount and duration of expected rainfall, and the capacity of the soil to absorb water and support vegetation. While the nylon fabric has the advantage of being permanent, the *fiber mat* is biodegradable and can be impregnated with grass seed before installation. Once the seeds have sprouted, the straw and coconut fibers act as mulch, protecting the vegetation until it has become fully established. Both products come in rolls and are easily installed with staples or pegs.

Since these products are mainly used in commercial applications, it may be difficult to find small amounts for residential use. Industry sources, however, indicate that a consumer-oriented product may be available sometime in the future.

Contour-wattling—installing woven twigs on a slope has been effectively used by the Soil Conservation Service to stabilize denuded hillsides and could easily be adapted for smaller sites. Wattle, an Anglo-Saxon word meaning interwoven twigs or branches, slows erosion in several ways. If installed with stakes and properly woven, it stabilizes slopes by reducing the sliding of topsoil and slowing the movement of water downhill. It traps sediments along the slope and increases the infiltration of water along a slope. And, by creating a suitable microclimate, the wattle itself will root, and thereby encourage the establishment of vegetative cover.

Willow is an ideal plant for wattling, since it is long and flexible and roots easily. Cut branches and bundle them together in uniform bunches of an eight- to ten-inch diameter. Install them in trenches one-half the diameter of the bunches and hold them in place on the downslope side by stakes driven through the wattles into the ground. Sometimes these stakes are

"live," being of the same material as the wattle itself. When they root, they will add more vegetative cover to the slope. Stakes should be placed about twelve to eighteen inches on center (apart), and driven into the ground perpendicular to the face of the hillside, extending about six inches above grade.

Wattle bunches should be woven so that butt or cut ends are toward the center of the bundle and the branch tips at either end. They should be tied at twelve- to fifteen-inch intervals. Start the installation procedure from the bottom of the slope and move upward. The best procedure to follow is to first drive a stake into the ground perpendicular with the slope. Trench above the stake and place the wattle in the trench so that about a third is exposed above grade. Secure the bundles with additional stakes and cover with soil, making sure the soil is firmly packed on top

of the bundles.

Another method of slope protection involves the insertion of live branches directly into the face of a slope. Called *brush layering,* this technique is used to stabilize fill slopes during construction. By altering the type of plants—using rooted cuttings rather than branches—you could adapt this method to a garden scale. This technique is similar to planting ground cover on a slope.

Stream banks can be stabilized effectively with *brush matting,* a technique that involves securing a mat of hardwood branches and brush along a bank with wire or stakes. Depending on the season and plant requirements, live cuttings of native trees or brush species that root easily are installed either before or after matting is laid. This method is employed when the possibility of erosion occurs from a stream, rather than from hillside runoff.

The use of fabric matting on this slope stabilizes the soil and allows a ground cover to root.

Structural Methods

There are many structural options available for stabilizing a hillside, each with its own advantages and limitations. *Gravity walls*, which retain the earth by their mass, are the most appropriate for residential applications. They can be built of wood, stone, brick, poured concrete, or concrete block (which are sometimes filled with concrete or rubble). *Retaining walls* must be able to support the weight of the earth they hold back when it is saturated; therefore, the higher the wall, the stronger it must be. If the wall is greater than two and one-half feet tall, special construction techniques (such as pouring a footer) will be needed, and a professional landscape architect should be consulted.

For small areas, railroad ties are easily and economically installed. These walls should be anchored by members imbedded directly into the slope and then secured to each other and into the ground by steel rods.

Stone is perhaps the most desirable material for garden retaining walls. Almost any kind of stone will work, and it can be laid in a variety of styles, depending on the desired effect. Many hillsides have rocks *in situ* that can be collected and used for a wall. Laying a wall with random-sized rocks is an art that requires some practice; the effects, however, are well worth the effort. (Don't forget that someone in your community may have much more experience at this than you do; hiring a local expert will probably produce a superior job and save you hours of trial and error.) It is not necessary to use mortar in stone walls, particularly if joints are tight. Slope the wall into the earth it is to retain and avoid continuous vertical joints. And don't forget that the interstices in a stone wall are ideal places for small plants or vines.

Poured-concrete or *concrete-block walls* are appropriate for larger walls, where strength, economy, and ease of installation are required. The strongest retaining wall is one of poured concrete, reinforced with rods or wire mesh. Hollow blocks can be laid rather easily, filled with concrete or rubble for strength, and then faced with a variety of finishes—stone, brick, paint, or stucco.

When planning a retaining wall, keep in mind that local materials (and building techniques) will probably be the easiest and most economical to use. Also remember that any wall must be pierced at regular intervals—horizontally and vertically—to allow accumulated moisture to escape. Installation of rubble or gravel behind the wall will allow water to drain quickly to these weep holes at the base of the wall.

Native stone is an attractive material for garden retaining walls. Not only is it found often on the site, but also it is easy to work with, particularly in a dry-wall construction such as this one.

CHAPTER FOUR

DESIGN IDEAS

HARMONIZING GARDEN FEATURES WITH PLANTS

When planning a hillside site, there are several different design directions to explore. As mentioned previously, you must first understand the site's environmental qualities: solar orientation, wind direction, soil characteristics, existing plant material, potential view, and so forth. Having done that, you can consider design possibilities.

If the site is heavily wooded, for instance, consider enhancing the setting by creating a garden of shade-loving plants. Narrow trails could meander through the site, bringing the visitor to hidden features, such as a small pond or garden structure. If the site is large enough, consider clearing an area to allow sunlight in, creating a contrast to the rest of the site.

If the site is cleared of trees, consider sowing it with a mixture of wildflowers. They will provide splashes of seasonal color and will be self-propagating. Another idea is to scatter spring bulbs—daffodils, snowdrops, and paperwhites—in great drifts up and down the hillside, a practice often seen in England.

Gently rolling hillside sites are ideal for orchards, vineyards, and vegetable plots—features that can occupy either an entire hill or a portion of the total site. Fruit trees, particularly apple and pear, are ideal for hillside planting. And anyone who has visited the wine-growing regions of America or Europe will recall how attractive a vineyard can be.

If a house is situated at the top of a hill, consider the placement of orchards and vegetable plots in relationship to the house: A deck or terrace for sitting should be close to the house, with vegetable plots, flower beds, or orchards below. Remember, too, the impact of a view looking down on a garden; whether the garden is decorative (a flower bed) or functional (a vegetable plot) the view will be an interesting feature.

If the site is relatively flat, it's best to use plants with rounded shapes and mounding forms to give the suggestion of an elevation change. Large shrubs, like rhododendron, and "weeping" tree forms, like weeping willow or European weeping beech, are possibilities for this effect. Introducing a strong vertical element in the planting—such as an Italian cypress, a white pine, or a Douglas fir—or espaliered specimens against a wall will reinforce a change of elevation by moving the eye upward. Fastigiate plant forms are such strong visual elements, though, and they should be used with restraint in spots where emphasis is desired.

When creating a garden with a view, choose the plant material carefully. Decide first whether the view is impressive enough to dominate the garden and, if so, keep the planting simple. Frame a view with trees or hedges and allow the foreground to be a green platform for the view.

With a sloping site, drainage considerations are necessarily a component of the design. Let this reality work as part of your design, rather than trying to ignore its existence. If, for instance, water collects after a heavy rain in a low spot at the base of your site, rather than trying to fill the spot to eliminate it, install plants that thrive in swampy situations and make it a feature of your design. The flow of water down your hillside could be manipulated and fed into a small stream lined with smooth rocks and planted with ferns and mosses.

At Thomas Jefferson's famed Monticello gardens, the vegetable plot is located at the base of a hill. Flat areas, or those with a slight slope, are best for vegetable gardens and fruit orchards.

STRUCTURAL FEATURES

*T*erraces, walls, and steps allow a hillside to be organized into a series of outdoor rooms, as previously discussed. Remember that the progression of spaces and visual features is of primary importance. Plan the sequence of these features to provide a variety of visual experiences, keeping in mind the precedents set by examples from the Italian Renaissance.

Progression of Slopes

*A*lthough they are individually unique, gardens of the Italian Renaissance share many of the same structural qualities. The backbone of these gardens is their strong circulation system.

The order of these gardens is reinforced by the progression of garden rooms, usually on levels going up or down a hill. Each room is self-contained, and, although a part of the whole, each room is complete within itself. Usually, these rooms had a specific function as well, acting as the locations for *al fresco* dining, outdoor entertaining, ceremonial and theatrical events, or just for strolling through and observing hedges and colorful plantings.

Keep in mind that large, level areas rarely exist on a sloping site. If the design of your garden requires flat areas for some function (such as a tennis court, vegetable plot, or pool), be prepared for the financial expenditure required to retain a space large enough—with walls or structures—for this activity.

The terraces, steps, and low walls of this section of Winterthur Garden in Delaware divide the space into a series of outdoor rooms and draw visitors' interest from one room to the next.

Terraces and Observation Sites

Remember that the top of a hillside is the part of the site most exposed to the elements—sun, wind, and rain. Therefore, structures or garden features should be located just below the crest of the hill, allowing some degree of protection from the elements.

A sloping site is enhanced by the employment of terraces for various garden functions or activities. The natural inclination on a hillside is to move down with the pull of gravity. Let that tendency work in your design, so that there is a progression of features or events to be experienced by movement down the slope.

Terraces, moving from the house down the hillside and constructed of materials compatible with the house, will help integrate the structure with the hillside. They can be organized to direct traffic to and from the house and they can define space for outdoor activities (such as sitting, viewing, and congregating). Terrace surfaces can be made of just about any material: grass, gravel, wood, brick, stone, or asphalt. Remember that large terraces are easy to walk across and are invitingly restful, encouraging the garden visitor to take time and linger, to sit, perhaps, and enjoy a view.

Platforms and terraces can emphasize the inherent drama of a hillside site, by allowing opportunities for the observation of the surrounding countryside. If the site is not steep enough to allow a sequence of terraces, consider constructing an observation tower or tree house for this function. It can double as a playhouse for the younger members of the family or a hidden retreat for private meditations. Let the tree house become a feature of your garden, making it an exercise in rustic architecture or a folly in the tradition of eighteenth-century England.

Constructed to complement its surroundings, this dwelling offers rooms for treetop living as well as opportunities for bird's-eye views of the surrounding landscape.

Built into the ground, this garden room is a private space that is sheltered from exposure to hilltop winds and sun.

Structure and natural planting can be harmoniously combined, as demonstrated by this deck, which is shaded and enhanced by a cloud of blooming crabapple.

Left: *Brick steps lend a formal, structured air to a garden.* **Right:** *Wood chips are an informal and natural material for a pathway.*

Steps

With a hillside view, steps are a necessary feature. Steps that occupy too much space should be avoided, however, since they will dominate the garden's overall design. Use steps—with associated retaining walls and landings—to give structure to the garden and to link one garden room with another.

Retaining walls and landings, often parts of a system of steps, can serve as viewing and seating platforms as well as locations for potted plants, sculpture, or water features. Think of landings as opportunities in the garden's circulation system to pause a moment and observe what lies ahead. By using material different from that of the pathway or steps leading to the landing and by making the landing larger than the pathway, the impact of the landing will be emphasized. Visually as well as function-

ally, the landing will be separate from what comes before and after it. Conversely, by using the same material in a landing as in the steps or path leading to it, and by keeping the landing dimensions similar or equal to those of the pathway, the landing's importance will be diminished, causing the garden visitor to move forward without stopping. Make the appropriate decision based on the specifics of your situation.

To highlight important views, plants, or features, make landings generous in size. Where these features do not occur, use small landings, with their function only to facilitate circulation.

When planning the connections between the top and bottom of the hillside site, several things should be kept in mind. You may need to move wheelbarrows and other garden equipment on a regular basis up and down the garden: In this case, a system of ramps may be more convenient than steps. Broad steps, with a deep tread

and a short riser, will allow easy movement of equipment yet will occupy a large amount of space. The dimensions of steps are calculated by the following rule: Twice the riser plus the tread should equal twenty-six. A gradual transition from one area to another should be made using a four-inch riser and an eighteen-inch tread. A greater vertical distance can accommodate risers of seven inches and treads of twelve inches.

For an unusual treatment of steep grade, particularly for an immediate effect in small areas that might wash away before erosion control can take hold, consider covering the slop with granite pavers. Set directly into the ground without any mortar, they can move around existing trees and will accommodate small ground covers in the interstices. This will provide an interesting contrast of material and textures with surrounding plantings and deck surfaces.

A flight of steps can separate garden

Above: A slight grade is emphasized by a change of ground material. These two garden rooms are distinct spaces, although the change in elevation between them is only several inches. Right: Wide steps made of railroad ties and gravel follow the gentle slope of the hillside. Steps like these promote leisurely walking.

Materials for Paths and Steps

Bricks—Used for paths and steps, bricks are a wonderful solution. Among the many patterns that can be used are running bond, basketweave, and herringbone. Most patterns, particularly in small areas, can be installed by the gardener with little trouble. For best results, lay brick in sand, using a level to ensure an even surface. For large areas, such as patios, terraces, or driveways, consider hiring a professional brick mason.

Concrete—This versatile material can be used for steps and paths, in poured form or in blocks. It can be washed in different colors. Consider placing leaves in wet cement. When it dries, the leaves will wash away, leaving behind an interesting pattern of "fossils." Concrete can also be topped with a pebble aggregate to provide a range of beautiful patterns.

Grass—This familiar ground cover can form a very attractive natural pathway in a formal or informal style, but must be frequently mown. Attractive when bordered by a meadow of wildflowers, it can also be cut as treads and paired with logs or railroad ties to form steps or ramps.

Gravel—A gravel path is the simplest type to construct and maintain. At least three inches of gravel are necessary to cut down on weeding. The edge of the gravel path is also an ideal seedbed. For surface interest, try gravel paths with contrasting sizes and colors of stone. Paths through woody gardens are best made of rustic materials—pine needles, woodchips, shredded bark, or leaves—as they provide a soft walking surface, and contribute nutrients to the soil. Be sure, in a "naturalistic" setting, to use indigenous material.

Stones—A path system may be paved with flat or slightly rounded stones, either slate, flagstone, or whatever is "found" on the site. Try laying them into the ground in an irregular pattern for a natural effect. A few carpeting plants such as thyme or ajuga can grow between them, softening uneven or straight edges.

Tile—Often seen in Japan and in Mediterranean-style gardens, tile lends a beautiful touch to paths and walls. Use the unglazed, quarry-paver type for groundwork and the more detailed, delicate varieties for ornamental touches, such as pool copings or wall decoration.

Wood—Use railroad ties or plank-style boardwalks for natural-looking but effective treads. Ties can be stacked on one another and anchored into the ground and each other with metal rods at regular intervals. Try to find old ties if possible, since the preservatives in new ties might leach into adjacent planting areas, causing harm.

rooms or, if broad and generous, bring two areas together. Narrow steps that do not reveal an obvious termination can induce movement by their mysterious nature. A completely different effect is achieved by broad steps that lead to a doorway or sculptural feature. They become a series of platforms leading in an ordered progression to a garden feature. Broad steps also can serve as retaining walls, creating an interesting and spacious terrace effect. A maze of footpaths and stone stairways may link a garden's levels. Native stone stairways can meander through weathered rock outcroppings, enhancing the garden's natural appearance.

Slightly elevated slopes can be protected from erosion through the use of timbers: These natural materials provide slope protection and also help define walking areas.

Fanciful Additions

Whether elevated or not, garden structures such as pergolas, gazebos, and belvederes are an ornamental asset to any garden. Used for centuries in gardens all over the world, these structures can be as ornamental as they are functional. They can echo the architecture of your house or they can be a completely unrelated architectural extravagance designed as a fanciful garden ornament.

If your site is large enough to have a series of hills, consider installing what is known in England as an "eyecatcher"—a Gothic ruin, a Grecian temple, or a piece of sculpture strategically placed so that the vista leading to it is a major part of the garden's design. In fact, some eighteenth-century English gardens, like Stourhead and Stowe, were composed of a series of these views, arranged in sequence through the garden. The visitor was expected to be familiar with the allegorical and philosophical references they evoked and to appreciate them not only for their beauty in the landscape but also for the classical references to which they alluded. These features carry the visitor's eye out into the garden and encourage the contemplation as well as the exploration of distant objects in the landscape.

A pergola is often connected to the house and will strengthen the transition between house and garden. Although generally roofless, the pergola's ceiling can also be created by vines, such as bouganvillea, clematis, Japanese wisteria, and climbing roses. Important considerations in plant selection are bloom, fra-

Left: *An arbor planted with wisteria will eventually bloom into a scented canopy that will shade garden visitors from the elements.* **Above:** *Ensconced in the trees of this garden is a pavilion that can only be reached by means of a small bridge. Its rooms overlook the woods and hillside below.*

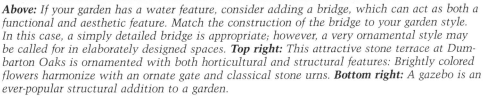

Above: If your garden has a water feature, consider adding a bridge, which can act as both a functional and aesthetic feature. Match the construction of the bridge to your garden style. In this case, a simply detailed bridge is appropriate; however, a very ornamental style may be called for in elaborately designed spaces. **Top right:** This attractive stone terrace at Dumbarton Oaks is ornamented with both horticultural and structural features: Brightly colored flowers harmonize with an ornate gate and classical stone urns. **Bottom right:** A gazebo is an ever-popular structural addition to a garden.

grance, and leaf cover. Keep in mind also that pergola plantings also require special pruning and maintenance activities.

The gazebo is another delightful garden addition. It can be constructed in many shapes and built of wood or ironwork. A square pavilion style is perhaps the most familiar, although some are circular, hexagonal, or octagonal structures. Victorian gazebos include structures with ornate cast-iron gingerbread or wooden scrollwork. Simple, rustic models made with rough-hewn logs are appropriate for natural-style gardens.

Belvederes or summerhouses tend to stand on their own as major structures. Generally, a belvedere is a structure from which a view is observed. A summerhouse often is a small cottage, strategically placed some distance from the main house. If your garden is large enough, a summerhouse could function as a convenient location for picnic supplies, garden furniture, and equipment.

Decks

Another useful garden structure is the deck. Particularly appropriate for hillside gardens, decks create a level space for outdoor activities and, when properly sited, afford the opportunity to take advantage of hillside views. Decks also can provide a transition from house into garden, adding interest to an otherwise ordinary exterior. Besides affording views or extending the living space from inside to out, decks provide a valuable garden asset in that they are a hard surface that can be built around trees without major disturbance to the roots below. Directly cover-

ing the area around a tree will disturb its ability to collect water and prevent air from getting to its roots; lack of water and air will ultimately kill a tree. Decks make it possible to build around a tree at an elevation that will allow normal drainage and aeration to occur, thereby avoiding harm to the tree. And, in some cases, decks can act as tree houses, allowing such treetop activities as bird-watching, children's play or the observation of garden spaces below.

Design of a deck is best left to a landscape architect, who can also advise about appropriate materials and finishes to use and features to include. Also, a deck designed by a professional should reflect an orderly and functional transition

from inside living space to outside: There should be a logical, functional, visual, and spatial flow from one space to another. A deck should bring the inside space out and allow the outside view to come in.

Decks can be designed with built-in features (like benches, storage areas, tables, hot-tubs, and barbecue grills) or they can be simple platforms with appropriate railings and movable furniture. They can be as simple or as detailed as necessary. Remember that the simpler the design, the easier it will be to construct. A simple design, however, need not be unfinished or rustic. Executed with well-resolved details, a simple deck is an expression of elegance and function and would be appropriate in just about any situation.

Decks not only create level spaces on hillsides but they also provide areas to view the landscape below.

A deck can level off sloped ground as well as provide space for outdoor activities.

When investigating property for purchase, keep in mind that steep sites are often available at reduced rates because of the perceived problems in hillside construction. With decks, however, outdoor living spaces can be enjoyed without actually having to be on the ground level, and a series of decks can be as interesting and special as any ground-level garden. Steep sites also suggest opportunities for innovative architecture for a residential structure that will include outdoor decks and platforms. In most cases, these sites will be wooded, and special precautions will have to be taken during construction to ensure that no damage occurs to existing trees. This cannot be stressed enough to both architect and builder. Following construction, however, little work will be necessary beyond removal of construction debris and basic repair to bring the ground plane back to its natural condition. Such sites are ideal for gardens of native and woodland plants. Consider allowing what exists to remain and adding a few shrubs or trees to the wooded site for special seasonal effects.

Decks are usually made of wood. Redwood is ideal because of its resistance to deterioration and its finished appearance. Other woods (red cedar, pine, cypress) can be used with appropriate preservative treatment, and pretreated lumber is readily available.

Water Systems

A sloping site offers the opportunity to exploit the various design possibilities and characteristics of water. Historical examples offer us inspiration: the water cascades at Chatsworth, England, the fountains of Villa Lante and Villa d'Este of Italy, and—from recent years—Lawrence Halprin's McIntyre Garden in California. Each one of these, in its own way, expresses a different possibility for water; and each gives an idea of how water features can be used in the hillside site.

Water has always played an important role in the gardens of hot countries. Other notable water gardens are found in India—at the water parterre at Amber, Jaipur, for example, water flows over a stone terrace, while a lake shimmers below. Ter-raced gardens also were established in the Indian country surrounding Lake Dal, where water from mountain springs flow down sloped hillsides.

Since many hillsides are adjacent to lakes or ponds, don't forget the reflective possibilities water provides. This is particularly important when siting a structure on your waterside property to take maximum advantage of all possible views.

Providing irrigation for your garden will ensure its survival through periodic dry spells. Irrigation systems can be as simple as a hose line and sprinkler or as elaborate as an automatic system with submerged lines and automatic timing. If your hillside garden is a half-acre or larger, strongly consider an automatic system. Although it may seem a luxury, such a system will pay for itself in convenience and time saved in just a few years.

Walls used to define different levels in a garden are ideal locations for major water features, such as this one at Nemours.

A water feature doesn't have to be large to be effective. This small pond, with its simple jet of water, is an uncomplicated means of introducing water into the garden on a limited scale.

This natural stream provides an ideal location for native ferns, mosses, and woodland plants.

At Old Westbury Garden on Long Island, the colorful impact of a bank of azaleas is magnified by their reflection in a pond.

ROCK GARDENS

Natural features of a site should be incorporated into—rather than eliminated from—a garden. Here, a preexisting rock outcrop is enhanced by low-growing plantings.

Situated in a low spot of the garden, these rocks are strategically placed to resemble a natural stream and to guide the flow of water.

In many parts of North America, rock outcroppings and glacial deposits of rock are commonly found in the landscape. Outcroppings are rock formations that appear at the surface of the ground, and since they are generally too large to move, they should be integrated into the design of your garden. Deposits of smaller rock are the result of glacial activity of thousands of years ago. Although sometimes visible on the surface of the ground, these deposits are often subsurface, and the extent of the deposits may come as a surprise to the gardener. Existence of outcroppings or subsurface deposits will certainly have an effect on the design of a hillside garden, the plants that are used, and the speed with which the garden progresses. While some subsurface deposits can easily be excavated and removed with hand tools, others will be too heavy and extensive to move and will simply have to remain. Before purchasing a hillside site, it would be advantageous to dig around at random locations, just to see what may exist below the ground's surface. Also, carefully observe adjacent property. If your neighbors' gardens are littered with rock and your site is not, you may safely assume that those on the surface have been removed, and you are likely to find many more in the ground.

Rocks that you remove from the soil can be used effectively as steps, retaining walls, or pathways in the garden. Excavating and moving subsurface rocks, however, is a time-consuming and arduous process; don't think of it as a weekend's task! Remember, too, that dry-wall rock construction is not as easy as it looks. For these garden tasks, it may be advisable to consider hiring experienced help.

If it is necessary to augment on-site rocks with those from somewhere else, strive for consistency in color, shape, and texture. Remember that nonnative stones may look out of place in your hillside garden. If using rock in a "natural" situation that does not include rock as a native element, choose the rock carefully with an eye toward the overall effect of introducing a foreign element into a natural setting. Another approach would be to emphasize the fact that this particular object—in this case a rock—does not exist in the site, yet the designer is including it as an object to look at and appreciate. Either way, let the planting and composition of the space suggest to the viewer which approach has been intended by the designer.

If sufficient quantities of "foreign" rock are used, however, and particularly if they are used architecturally for walls, terraces, and structures, placement becomes less important. Using large quantities of the same kind of rock can link structures, such as walls and buildings, with the landscape in an organic and satisfying way.

Rocks can also be used as erosion protection and slope stabilizers. Either regularly shaped stones (such as granite sets) or irregular rocks can be used. Firmly "plant" them in the slope, leaving about one-third or less of the rocks' thickest parts exposed. If using regularly shaped rocks, leave a uniform space (one to three inches) between each space to allow room for a ground cover. If using irregular shapes, vary the interstices to allow for the planting of different varieties of ground covers. Use larger stones at the foot of the slope and smaller ones toward the top. Leave spaces in between for plants, and remember that the addition of just about any plant will contribute to the stabilization of a slope. Check plants in "Resources" (page 88) for suggestions for your area.

Pockets in rocks can be planted with small plants, such as gypsophila, left, and dianthus, right.

This rock garden is dramatized by the use of plants with rich, seasonal color. Steps guide the garden visitor around the rocks, each step providing a different observation point.

CHAPTER FIVE

TWO HILLSIDE GARDENS

Hillside gardens can be large or small, simple or grand. They can require the work of an army of gardeners, or the dedication of a couple's weekend time. The following two examples of hillside gardens—the Jansma garden in Fayetteville, Arkansas, and Dumbarton Oaks in Washington, D.C.—offer an examination of two extremes. Just about every aspect of these two gardens is different: Where Dumbarton Oaks is grand and structured, the Jansma garden is small and constantly evolving with the couple's changing lifestyle and horticultural interests. While Dumbarton Oaks is the product of an established plan—recorded instructions about what to plant and how each space should look—the Jansmas try something new each growing season and do all the work themselves.

With the many differences in these two gardens, however, there are important similarities. Both are the products of intelligent and dedicated planning, and both demonstrate the result of love and careful attention. Both are resources for other gardeners, as well, and provide inspiration for any garden situation, whether it is on a hillside or not.

Left: *The Jansma garden boasts an attractive iris border.* **Right:** *The vegetable garden is situated to take advantage of sun.*

AN OZARK MOUNTAIN GARDEN

Jerome and Harriet Jansma purchased their Fayetteville, Arkansas house a decade and a half ago, complete with a nearby lot and a steep Ozark southern slope surrounding the house. Although they could already appreciate the natural beauty of the site and felt justified in calling it a "garden," the couple felt compelled to develop their property further.

They did have some preexisting landscaping to build on: For twenty-five years others had lived there, and although none had pursued the art of gardening with great zeal, they all had contributed to the shape of the landscape. One former resident had built an extensive network of sandstone dry walls to retain and shape the sandy loam native to the site; more recent owners had allowed the free growth of a mixed hardwood forest mostly composed of oak trees, which now provides shade for the house. Previous owners had also cleared the lot below, where the Jansmas were later to develop a vegetable plot, flower garden, and orchard.

The layout that the Jansmas began with was as follows: The house was set into the hill and surrounded by steep terraces with narrow pathways running between them. The gently sloping lower lot had been terraced. Assessing this house layout, they set to work calculating the important technical aspects of hillside gardening—through observation.

They watched the sun's progression through its yearly cycle, to see where the shadows fell; they determined where desirable vistas lay; and they identified through the year where to screen off and where to enhance the site's surroundings.

The owners began to realize that spatial relationships were already provided for them, naturally suggested by the topography and the plantings. Pines and native cedars seemed to frame and enhance their view to the south of the Boston Mountains, and the protective framework of stone walls, terraces, and tall oaks made the dwelling and its near yard feel enclosed, further emphasizing the long vistas. Terraces and a level table of land below seemed to be waiting for plantings—the terraces ready for dwarf apple trees and perennial borders; the table for a vegetable plot that is also planted with bright annual flowers. The various elevations added interest to the landscape and required no alteration. The couple notes, ''We did not have the task that for many gardeners is the most difficult, that of creating depth and interesting perspectives in a garden. They were simply there.''

Much of the work of the site was accomplished by the Jansmas alone. The steep and rocky site was covered with a thin soil and could only be gardened with hand tools. Even in the level vegetable garden, huge, flat sandstones lay just under the surface; and no planting hole could be dug with a spade. Instead, picks and mattocks were the standard hand tools. In one years's time, they excavated enough stone from the vegetable plot alone to line the lower garden lot with a dry wall two and one-half feet high as well as build an eight-foot-high retaining wall along the streetside in front of the house.

To pave the pathways that ran between the steeply sloping terraces above and behind the house, a combination of wood chips and sawdust—available from local wood-processing industries—was used. These natural materials allow for soft and easy treading while also enabling much-needed rainfall to penetrate the soil.

''Sloping gardens drain faster than flat ones, and all gardeners of hillside sites must be attentive to this potential problem,'' Harriet Jansma advises. Newly planted trees and shrubs and herbaceous perennials must have adequate water, and gardeners must be realistic about this fact. You cannot carry buckets of water up and down hills or drag hoses around forever. Even in an area like northwest Arkansas where yearly rainfall is plentiful—averaging forty-eight inches—there are hot, dry periods in summer and periods of drought in winter, when snow cover does

not always protect plants in times of severe cold.

Like many gardeners, the Jansmas at first resisted the idea of a garden of native plants, which already existed to some degree on the spot. Following more fashionable planting schemes, they planted the species they thought every Southern garden must have, such as azaleas, rhododendrons, roses, and flowering plants. Yet in dry places, very few ornamental plants can survive.

Their long-term solution has been to rely on native plants: to let grow the trees and other plants that already live on the site; to add and subtract from their number only when a particular spot is to be enhanced. The native trees are, therefore, the backbone of the garden. Having learned from their earlier mistakes, these Ozark Mountain gardeners now boast a shade garden that does not compete with the distant views below but, rather, frames them and provides lush, deep greens and coolness.

Gardeners can also determine which plants will grow successfully on their sites by consulting reference books that describe plants native to their area. The Jansmas used books like *Trees of Arkansas* by Dwight M. Moore and *Missouri Wildflowers* by Edgar Denison to identify their own native plants and find others that would likely succeed on their site. Similar print resources are available for every region of the country, and many areas have local native plant societies (see ''Resources'' page 93). These owners used their local resources to survey the site, and listed its species in order to avoid destroying any planting that already thrived and enhanced the property.

Slow change coupled with careful observation has enhanced the garden in other ways. As changes were cautiously made, views emerged or were improved through natural framings of plantings. A thicket in the southwest corner of the lower garden lot has screened a huge city water tank from view, while an adolescent evergreen forest screens out the harsh light of a mercury-vapor street lamp to the south-

Natural areas of this Ozark Mountain garden feature native plants and wildflowers.

east, allowing clearer viewings of moon rises on long summer evenings.

Existing structural screens also served well to give privacy. To the west, the garage screens a small rock patio from the view of passersby, making the seating space near the slope almost totally private and turning the Ozark cliffdwellers' lot into an outdoor living room, enclosed by the stone wall behind and by the house and garage to the sides. The retaining wall just below the house, along the street, provides space not only for the tiny herb garden and pool that now form the near view from the indoor living room, but also for a secret bench—which, protected from the street by a huge Eastern red cedar (*Juniperus virginiana*), provides views miles into the mountains. The ordinary red cedar is one mainstay of this hillside garden, especially impressive beside the steep, narrow rock steps that climb the hill east of the house.

Another well-learned garden lesson has been that closing views can create an element of surprise. Both plantings and structured features are arranged to draw visitors into the varied garden spaces, leading them from one area to another for interest and contrast. "Our future development of the garden will concentrate on creating more enclosures, defining more outdoor rooms and creating more areas within the one and one-half acre space where we can rest and feel at home," notes Mrs. Jansma.

In addition to the patio to the west, a swing nearby, and the previously mentioned wooden bench to the south of the house on its east side, the upper site naturally provided many places to sit. Nearly every preexisting rock wall could be sat upon; and only one new wall for sitting needed to be constructed—a large one that encloses the herb garden just outside the front wall. Like other seat walls, it is eighteen inches tall, the standard height for comfortable seating.

Places to sit and contemplate did not exist in the lower garden when the owners first arrived, and they have only begun to provide them. The steps there, which are

A shady path leads from the Jansma's house to the terrace overlooking their hillside garden. The view is to the south.

made of new railroad ties, are wide and generous and make surprisingly comfortable outdoor seats.

Another surprising garden element has been the unexpected, spontaneous use of one spot in the garden as a modest theater—in the style of Italian outdoor "theater" gardens of the past—by creative and inspired neighborhood children. A large, sturdy bench—about the size of a double bed—became their stage, the nearby steps providing seats for an audience. This steel-framed wooden platform has proved such a success that it was followed by a smaller one of the same structural design, placed behind the house. Directly set into the soil behind a rock dry wall, it overlooks the top of the house and the oak trees to the distant hills. It has the feeling of a crow's nest on a ship, soaring far above the surrounding terrain.

Future plans call for more seating and construction. On the east end of the lower garden sits a rectangular shed where larger tools are stored. A very plain wooden porch will be attached to it, with a short, shallow ramp for rolling carts and a mower into the shed, and a place for resting in the shade of the pines. On the opposite end of the lot, seating plans are less exact; however, ambitious plans for a new structure are developing, partly because—as luck would have it—stones are piling up again. The Jansmas envision a small stone building for this southwest corner, with a sunny paved eating area to the south of it; its south edge will be closed off to wind and view by a high "stone curtain" wall with one small, high window—a secret garden for sunning.

In its constant state of development and gentle revision, the Jansma garden is a model that can inspire and teach other would-be hillside gardeners. Here simple structures such as sheds, benches, and paths work together with natural plantings to form a hillside garden environment that seems as timeless as the Ozark mountains themselves.

In the foreground of the house, bulbs and native grasses form a dense carpet under fruit trees.

DUMBARTON OAKS

The lines of the retaining wall at the west end of the swimming pool are softened by branches of white azalea.

Dumbarton Oaks is one of the finest gardens in America—a living textbook of what to do with a hillside site. Like many other outstanding examples of garden design throughout history, it represents the combined efforts of a talented designer, an enthusiastic and wealthy client, and a spectacular site. Dumbarton Oaks is a garden of many rooms and many moods. As a source of design ideas, it is an inspiration for any garden enthusiast. Dumbarton Oaks is a special place that gives its visitor something new to consider at each visit. Examination of how these spaces were designed, how they have aged, and how plants are used as an integral part of the design are a good representation of how to approach a hillside garden.

The design of Dumbarton Oaks is the work of Beatrix Jones Farrand. She had important commissions and clients during her career (among them the Rockefellers and Yale University) and was one of the founders of the American Society of Landscape Architects (ASLA), yet the significance of her work only recently has been recognized.

Beatrix Farrand was born in 1872 to a family of wealth and social standing in New York City and she benefited from the cosmopolitan exposure and European travel her family could afford. Introduced at an early age to gardening, she left New York in 1898 and moved to the Boston area to study horticulture with Professor Charles S. Sargent, at that time considered to be the dean of American horticulture. Professor Sargent was the director of the Arnold Arboretum, and he suggested she pursue a career in landscape design. It was from Professor Sargent that Beatrix Farrand learned about plants—knowledge that would have a profound influence on her later work. Professor Sargent advised her "to make the plan fit the ground and not twist the ground to fit a plan." He further advised her to travel in Europe, to see as many gardens as possible and to study landscape painting. The effect of this advice can easily be seen in all her work, particularly in the garden at Dumbarton Oaks.

In 1920, Mildred Bliss and her husband purchased a grand but somewhat dilapidated farmhouse estate in the Georgetown section of Washington, D.C., in anticipation of establishing a permanent residence following his retirement from the diplomatic service. The house was built in 1801 and is Georgian in conception. It sits on a rather high hill above Rock Creek, on property that was blessed with a substantial change of topography and a generous growth of mature trees, including oaks, elms, beeches, maples, tulip trees, and sycamores. The house faces south, with a generous front lawn that gently slopes down to the street. The simple treatment of the front—lawn, mature trees, and evergreen shrubs—is an appropriate setting for the majestic simplicity of the structure. Major garden developments are to the rear (north) and side (east) of the house. Along the western side of the property are buildings housing the famous Garden Library of Dumbarton Oaks, its Byzantine Collection, and the Pre-Columbian Collection. These facilities, as well as the garden, are open to the public. Maintenance and service areas are also located on this side.

The main garden begins in the rear of the house with the North Vista, created by four descending lawn terraces, which are on axis with the main entrance to the house. Conceived as outdoor spaces for entertaining, each terrace is a different shape and size. They gradually narrow to a semicircular point of observation, thereby creating the effect of a false perspective. This visual device, borrowed from the architects of the Italian Renaissance, increases the apparent depth of the vista. The impact of the North Vista is further enhanced by the "borrowed view" of the adjacent countryside, which allows

Above: *Dumbarton Oaks is composed of many areas that incorporate different types of landscape techniques. The Ellipse is an open space of closely mown lawn.* ***Middle:*** *Forsythia Hill uses mass plantings of shrubbery.* ***Below:*** *Through shape, size, and use of material, the Horseshoe Steps lend importance and visual interest to this space in the garden.*

the garden to extend beyond the boundaries of its property line. When viewed from the house, the North Vista appears as a large stretch of lawn extending out into the wooded distance of Rock Creek. Viewed from the opposite end toward the house, the brick risers of the turfed steps merge, linking the brick of the house with the structure of the garden.

To the east of the house is a series of terraced garden "rooms," beginning with the Orangery, which is attached to the house. It originally housed ferns and tropical plants, and it opens onto a path that leads to the Beech Terrace. A simple panel of ground covers and bulbs is planted under the great American beech that fills this space. The Beech Terrace overlooks the Box or Urn Terrace, which features a large stone urn. This terrace was intended as an introduction to the Rose Garden, on a level about twelve feet below. In order for the Rose Garden to be as large as possible, the Urn Terrace is rather narrow. The original design of low-growing boxwood hedges and grass panels has been replaced by a design featuring scrolls of ground cover outlining intricately patterned pebble beds.

The Rose Garden is the largest terrace of the entire development. With a combination planting of roses and boxwood bushes, its design is formal, with the roses grouped together by color. Two flights of stairs lead from the Rose Terrace to the Fountain Terrace. Overlooks and landings allow opportunities to observe the space below with its two small pools and fountains. This terrace was envisioned by Farrand as "the one real flower garden in the series of terraces." In her instructions for its maintenance, Farrand wrote, "This garden is the one in which most change and replacement is necessary, in order to keep up the blooming effect throughout the season, and any alternation in the scheme permitting this blooming effect throughout the season would seem a mistaken economy." It is in this garden, too, that we see how strongly Beatrix Farrand was influenced by the writings and work of Gertrude Jekyll, the important English garden designer of the late-nineteenth century.

A few steps below the Fountain Terrace is the Arbor Terrace, originally intended to be an intimate, secluded garden. To minimize the "overwhelming height"—as Beatrix Farrand described it—of the stone wall required to retain the corner of the Rose Garden above it, an arbor modified from the design of DuCerceau was installed. Built of cypress, it supports a covering of wisteria and is spectacular in the spring. A steep slope north and east of this terrace is retained by a wall, and from an observation point on the northern side, one looks through an aerial hedge of pear trees to the herbaceous border garden beyond. This slope, in Beatrix Farrand's words, should be "clothed in fruit trees, not only for their own beauty but for the purpose of hiding a steep slope and bolstering the northeast end of the Herb Garden" (now the Arbor Terrace).

These terraced rooms, with their accompanying steps, are as Farrand put it, "conspicuously narrow." Their design, however, reflects "the surrounding natural levels both to the north and south of these terraces, as nearly as possible, so that the big trees on either side would not be destroyed in carrying out the garden design." Each room is contained within itself, and each has its own character, personality, and plant palette.

To the southeast of the Fountain Terrace is the Lovers' Lane Pool, with its adjacent grassy amphitheater. This room is at the easternmost boundary of the garden's property and is approximately fifty-five feet below the level of the Orangery. Farrand reported that, like the terraces above it, this space was "entirely controlled by the natural slope of the ground and the desire to keep as many of the native trees as possible unhurt and undisturbed."

The Pebble Garden, composed of Mexican beach pebbles of different sizes and colors, is designed to be viewed from above. The shallow expanse of water heightens this effect.

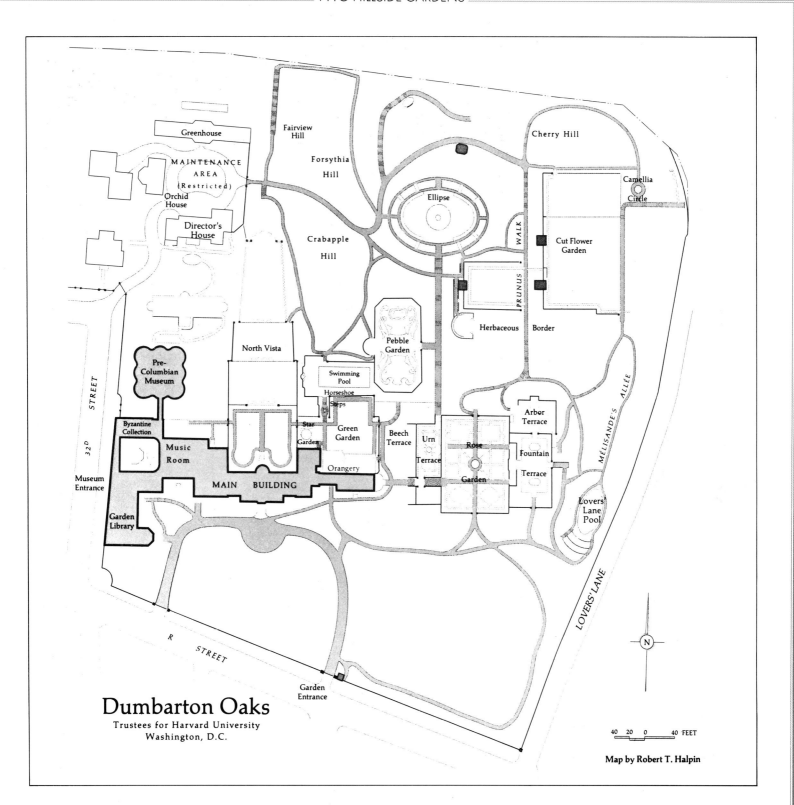

Greenhouse

MAINTENANCE AREA (Restricted)

Orchid House

Director's House

Fairview Hill

Forsythia Hill

Crabapple Hill

Cherry Hill

Ellipse

Camellia Circle

Cut Flower Garden

PRUNUS WALK

Herbaceous Border

North Vista

Pre-Columbian Museum

Pebble Garden

Swimming Pool

Horseshoe Steps

Byzantine Collection

Music Room

Star Garden

Green Garden

Beech Terrace

Urn Terrace

Rose Garden

Arbor Terrace

Fountain Terrace

MÉLISANDE'S ALLÉE

Museum Entrance

32ᴰ STREET

MAIN BUILDING

Orangery

Lovers Lane Pool

Garden Library

LOVERS' LANE

R STREET

Garden Entrance

Dumbarton Oaks

Trustees for Harvard University
Washington, D.C.

40 20 0   40 FEET

Map by Robert T. Halpin

N

Other major garden rooms include the Green Garden, the Swimming Pool and Pebble Garden (formerly a tennis court), and the Ellipse, all of which are north of the Orangery. The Green Garden is dominated by a large black oak, underplanted with various ground covers. The northern edge is a balustrade that overlooks the swimming pool below and forms the structure for the pool's loggia. Adjacent to the pool is the Pebble Garden, which, like other areas of the garden, was designed to be viewed from above. It is an elaborately patterned mosaic of stones and shells, covered with a shallow sheet of water.

The Ellipse lies at the terminus of a pathway descending from the Urn Terrace. It is an elliptical expanse of closely mown lawn, originally designed to be surrounded by a wall of clipped boxwood, fifteen to twenty-five feet high. This was removed in 1958 and replaced by a hedge of clipped American hornbeam, giving the space a much more architectural feeling. In the center of the lawn is an antique French fountain, bought for the garden in the late 1920s and relocated from its original site, the present location of the building that houses the Pre-Columbian Collection (located on the western side of the property, in a building designed by Philip Johnson).

Around all of these ''rooms'' are loosely structured spaces, designed as both separations and transitions between the formal areas. There is an orchard of pear and apple trees beyond the Arbor Terrace, mass plantings of shrubbery in the Forsythia Hill, and hillsides devoted to groups of cherry trees (Cherry Hill) and crabapple trees (Crabapple Hill). In the lowest part of the garden is a naturalistic park that leads to Rock Creek, an area that was originally part of the garden but was deeded to the National Park Service in 1940.

Throughout the garden, the visitor is drawn from one ''room'' to the next by the anticipation of what lies ahead and by the expectation of what is beyond. This movement is achieved partially by the naturally

The stone retaining wall was built at the greatest point of natural elevation change in the garden. The Rose Garden is above; the Fountain Terrace, with its two small pools sunk into the grassy floor, is below.

A detail of steps reveals how brick risers and grass treads provide a transition from one level to another.

descending slope of the ground plane; but it is enhanced by the skillful use of plants to define spaces and to establish different moods and by the system of walkways that connect each "room." Straight and generously proportioned surfaces connect the more formal rooms in an ordered sequence, while curving narrow pathways are used in the more natural areas. This system of circulation promotes a variety of viewing sequences and allows the visitor to experience the rooms of the garden in many different orders.

There are many lessons to be learned from Dumbarton Oaks. Our major interests here has been to investigate how a hillside garden can be designed as a series of rooms, each with its own special character and feeling and to learn the importance of plant materials in the design of a garden. Each plant was used for a specific purpose and to achieve a desired effect. We are fortunate that Mrs. Farrand's intentions, and her thoughts about what the garden should be, have been recorded and recently published (*Beatrix Farrand's Plant Book for Dumbarton Oaks*, 1980). By carefully studying these notes, we can more fully understand the purpose the designer envisioned for each space. And finally, Dumbarton Oaks teaches us the importance of details in a garden. The impact of a paving pattern, the width of a pathway or of a terrace balustrade, the placement of a bench to facilitate a special view—all of these are vital to the success of a garden, and they are expressed nowhere better than in the gardens of Dumbarton Oaks.

Dumbarton Oaks is located at 1703 32nd Street Northwest, Washington, D.C. It is closed on national holidays. For further information call (202) 338-8278.

The Arbor Terrace provides a spectacular view to the north.

FINAL WORDS

Throughout the life of your hillside garden—from the initial design process through the construction stages and into its seasonal changes—remain observant. Make notes, mental as well as written, on what works and what doesn't; keep accounts of what you purchase, from whom it comes, and how well it does. Keep a file of interesting garden details or illustrations of ideas to try from newspapers, magazines, or garden books. Be creative when adapting these ideas to your own situation.

If an idea or a plant does not work, don't despair; experiment with something different! A garden is a livng—and therefore changing—space. Let its growth reflect your growth.

Remember that a garden is more than just a collection of plants artfully or functionally arranged, and it is more than an extension of your house. It is an expression of your interests and your personality. It is an opportunity to create beauty and to renew your acquaintance with nature.

RESOURCES

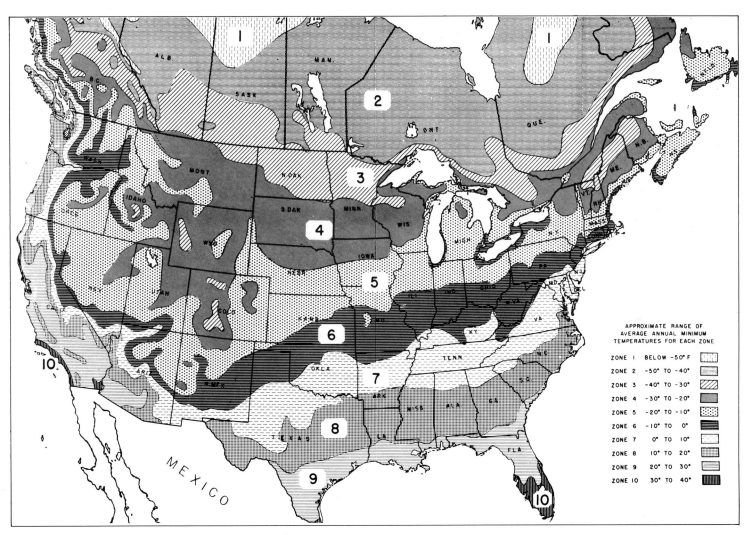

The Zones of Plant Hardiness

SUGGESTED PLANTS

The following are plant suggestions for a hillside garden. This is by no means an all-encompassing list: It includes a variety of plants that will grow in a wide range of hillside situations. Most plants, with the obvious exceptions of those that require specialized growing conditions, will grow on a hillside, assuming requirements for soil composition, exposure, and moisture are met. As mentioned in the text, it is strongly suggested that primary consideration in plant selection be given to natives of your region, since they are acclimated to localized conditions and are probably more readily available.

In compiling the following lists, consideration was given to a variety of plant characteristics: form and habit of growth; geographic availability and adaptability; leaf or bark texture; seasonal interest in leaf or flower; ability to attract wildlife; and year-round appearance. Numbers following some plant names refer to zones of hardiness.

Before making final decisions about plant selections, do some research on what plantings would be appropriate for your specific conditions. Consult your local nursery, library, or native plant society to find a reference appropriate to your region. Remember, too, that local nurseries can suggest varieties or hybrids that are suited to specific growing conditions.

Bulbs

Crocus spp.	Crocus
Narcissus Jonquilla	Jonquil
Narcissus	
Pseudonarcissus	Daffodil
Narcissus Tazetta	Narcissus
Tulipa Gesnerana	Tulip

Ground covers

Ajuga reptans	Ajuga	7
Cotoneaster spp.	Cotoneaster	6–9
Epigaea repens	Trailing Arbutus	3–8
Erica herbacea	Spring Heath	5–7
Hedera helix	English Ivy	4
Helleborus niger	Christmas Rose	8
Hosta plantaginea	Hosta	3–9
Galium odoratum	Sweet Woodruff	5–9
Lavandula angustifolia	English Lavender	6–8
Liriope muscarii	Liriope	6
Pachysandra terminalis	Pachysandra	5–7
Santolina spp.	Lavender Cotton	6
Sedum acre	Gold Moss	4
Trifoloim incarnatum	Crimson Clover	
Trillium spp.	Trillium	5
Vinca major	Periwinkle	6
Vinca minor	Littleleaf Periwinkle	4

Rock-garden plants

For crevices in rock walls, plantings in rock gardens, or along stone paths, the following plants are suggested:

Acantholimon spp.	Thrift
Achillea spp.	Dward Yarrow
Aethionema spp.	Stone-Cress
Aquilegia spp.	Columbine
Calluna vulgaris	Heather
Campanula spp.	Campanula
Chrysanthemum spp., Anthemis tribe	Alpine Chrysanthemum
Daphne spp.	Daphne
Dianthus spp.	Rock Pinks
Erica spp.	Heath
Gentiana spp.	Gentian
Geranium spp.	Geranium
Helianthemum spp.	Sun Rose
Hepatica spp.	Hepatica
Hypericum spp.	St.-John's-Wort
Iberis spp.	Candytuft
Myosotis alpestris	Alpine-Forget-Me-Not
Phlox spp.	Rock Phlox
Primula spp.	Primrose
Saxifraga spp.	Saxifrage
Sedum spp.	Sedum
Thymus spp.	Thyme
Vaccinium spp.	Dwarf Blueberry

Shrubs

Deciduous Types

Cytisus scoparius	Scotch Broom	6–9
Forsythia intermedia	Border Forsythia	4–8
Forsythia suspensa	Weeping Forsythia	
Hamamelis virginiana	Witch Hazel	4–9
Hydrangea macrophylla	Bigleaf Hydrangea	6–9
Hydrangea quercifolia	Oakleaf Hydrangea	5–9
Jasminum nudiflorum	Winter Jasmine	6–9
Philadelphus coronarius	Mock Orange	2
Rhus typhina	Staghorn Sumac	3–8
Rosa rugosa	Rugosa Rose	3–7
Rosa wichuriana	Memorial Rose	5–9
Syringa vulgaris	Lilac	3
Viburnum dentatum	Arrowwood	4–9

Evergreen Types

Elaeagnus pungens	Thorny Elaeagnus	7–9
Ilex aquifolium	English Holly	7–9
Ilex cassine	Dahoon Holly	7–9
Illicium anisatum	Japanese Anise Tree	8–9
Jasminum floridum	Florida Jasmine	7
Juniperus horizontalis 'Bar Harbor'	Bar Harbor Juniper	3–8
Kalmia latifolia	Mountain Laurel	5–9
Leucothoë fontanesiana	Drooping Leucothoë	
Ligustrum sinense	Chinese Privet	7
Pyracantha coccinea	Pyracantha	6
Rhododendron catawbiense	Catawba Rhododendron	5–7
Rhododendron maximum	Rosebay Rhododendron	
Taxus baccata	English Yew	6
Taxus canadensis	American Yew	2
Taxus cuspidata	Japanese Yew	4

Trees

Deciduous Types

Acer rubrum	Red Maple	3–9
Acer saccharum	Sugar Maple	3–9
Fagus grandiflora	American Beech	3–9
Fagus sylvatics 'Fastigiata'	European Beech	3–9
Gymnocladus dioica	Kentucky Coffee Tree	3–8
Juglans cinerea	Butternut	3–7
Juglans nigra	Eastern Black Walnut	4–9
Liquidambar styraciflua	Sweet Gum	5–9
Liriodendron tulipifera	Tulip Tree	4–9
Magnolia grandiflora	Southern Magnolia	5–9
Magnolia macrophylla	Bigleaf Magnolia	5–9
Oxydendrum arboreum	Sourwood	5–9
Populus alba	White Poplar	4
Quercus alba	White Oak	3–9
Quercus falcata	Southern Red Oak	7
Quercus palustris	Pin Oak	4–8
Quercus prinus	Chestnut Oak	4
Quercus rubra maxima	Eastern Red Oak	4–8

Evergreen Types

Cedrus atlantica	Atlas Cedar	6
Cedrus deodora	Deodar Cedar	7
Cryptomeria japonica	Cryptomeria	6–9
Cupresses sempervirens	Italian Cypress	8
Ilex attenuata 'Fosteri'	Foster's Holly	
Ilex opaca	American Holly	
Juniperus virginia 'Hillspire'	Eastern Red Cedar	3–9
Picea abies	Norway Spruce	2
Picea pungens	Colorado Spruce	3–7
Pinus nigra	Black Pine	4–8
Pinus parviflora	Japanese White Pine	4–7
Pinus resinosa	Norway Pine	3–6
Pinus strobus	Eastern White Pine	3–8
Pinus taeda	Loblolly Pine	7–9
Pinus virginiana	Virginia Pine	5–9
Thuja placata	Giant Arborvitae	4–7

Small-Flowering Deciduous Types

Aesculus glabra	Ohio Buckeye	4
Aesculus pavia	Red Buckeye	6
Cercis canadensis	Redbud	5–9
Chionanthus virginia	Fringe Tree	5
Cornus florida	Dogwood	5–8
Cornus kousa	Chinese Dogwood	5–7
Crataegus phaepyrum	Washington Hawthorn	4
Halesia carolina	Carolina Silverbell	5–9
Prunus serrulata	Oriental Cherry	6–8
Prunus subhirtella 'Pendula'	Weeping Cherry	5
Pyrus calleryana 'Bradford'	Bradford Pear	5–9

Vines

Celastrus scandens	Bittersweet
Gelseminum sempervirens	Caroling Yellow Jessamine
Lonicera japonica	Japanese Honeysuckle
Lonicera sempervirens	Trumpet Honeysuckle
Parthenocissus quinquefolia	Virginia Creeper
Parthenocissus tricuspidata	Boston Ivy
Smilax hispida	Southern Smilax
Wisteria floribunda	Japanese Wisteria

Wildflowers

This list includes a wide variety of annual and perennial species adapted to a range of environmental conditions. Wildflower seeds are commercially produced and available through retail nurseries and plant suppliers. Check with your landscape architect or local nursery for sources.

Northeastern Region

Achillea millefolium	Yarrow
Asclepias tuberosa	Butterfly Weed
Coreopsis lanceolata	Lance-Leaved Coreopsis
Digitalis purpurea	Foxglove
Gypsophila muralis	Baby's Breath
Oenothera lamarckiana	Evening Primrose
Rudbeckia hirta	Black-Eyed Susan

Southeastern Region

Aschleias tuberosa	Butterfly Weed
Chrysanthemum leucanthemum	Shasta Daisy
Coreopsis tinctoria	Plains Coreopsis
Cosmos sulphureua	Sulphur Cosmos
Echinacea purpurea	Purple Coneflower
Liatris pycnostachya	Prairie Blazing Star
Linaria maroccana	Toadflax
Phlox drummondii	Phlox
Rudbeckia amphexicaulis	Coneflower

Rocky Mountain Region

Aquilegia coerulea	Rocky Mountain Columbine
Aster tanacetifolius	Prairie Aster
Chrysanthemum leucanthemum	Oxeye Daisy
Gilia capitata	Globe Gilia
Linum lewisii	Blue Flax
Papaver nudicaule	Iceland Poppy
Penstemon spp.	Penstemon
Rudbeckia hirta	Black-Eyed Susan

California Region

Cheiranthus allionii	Wallflower
Clarkia unguiculata	Mountain Garland
Coreopsis tinctoria	Plains Coreopsis
Delphinium cardinale	Scarlet Larkspur
Dimorphotheca sinuata	African Daisy
Gilia leptantha purposii	Showy Blue Gilia
Linanthus grandiflorus	Mountain Phlox
Lupinus vallicola	Valley Lupine
Mentzelia lindleyi	Blazing Star
Nemophila maculata	Five Spot
Papaver rhoeas	Corn Poppy
Phacelia campanularia	Bluebells
Sisyrinchium bellum	Blue-Eyed Grass

Southwestern Region

Achillea millefolium	Yarrow
Aster tanacetifolius	Prairie aster
Chrysanthemum carinatur	Painted Daisy
Coreopsis tinctoria	Plains Coreopsis
Eschscholzia californica	California Poppy
Lupinus succulentus	Arroyo Lupine
Phacelia campanularia	Bluebells
Ratibida columnaris	Mexican Hat
Verbena tenuisecta	Moss Verbena

Pacific Northwest Region

Alyssum sacatile	Golden Turf
Centaurea cyanus	Dwarf Cornflower
Clarkia amoena	Farewell-To-Spring
Collinsia heterophylla	Chinese Houses
Digitalis purpurea	Foxglove
Eschscholzia californica	California Poppy
Gilia tricolor	Bird's-Eye
Linum lewisii	Blue Flax
Nemophilia menziesii	Baby Blue-Eyes
Oenothera lamarckiana	Evening Primrose
Papaver nudicaule	Iceland Poppy

Midwestern Region

Ammi majus	Bishop's Flower
Aster tanacetifolois	Prairie Aster
Coreopsis lanceolata	Lance-Leaved Coreopsis
Gaillardia aristata	Blanketflower
Gypsophilia muralis	Baby's Breath
Linaria maroccana	Toadflax
Monarda citriodora	Lemon Mint
Oenothera missouriensis	Missouri Primrose
Petalostemum purpureum	Purple Prairie Clover
Phlox drummondii	Phlox
Rudbeckia hirta	Black-Eyed Susan

INDEX

Page numbers in italics refer to captions, illustrations, and sidebars.

PICTURE CREDITS

Allan Brown: 74

Karen Bussolini: 39*(t)*

Langdon Clay: 58

John Deane: 42

Rene Diaz: 25*(bl)*

William Lake Douglas: 25*(br)*, 75*(br)*

Susan M. Duane: 10, 43*(t)*

Courtesy of Dumbarton Oaks: 83

Courtesy of Environmental Seed Producers: 31*(bl)*

Derek Fell: 12–13, 14, 17, 21, 22*(l and r)*, 24, 25*(tl)*, 28, 29, 33*(t and b)*, 35, 38*(t and b)*, 39*(b)*, 40*(bl and br)*, 41*(b)*, 45, 46, 48, 49, 50, 50–51, 51*(br)*, 52*(r)*, 53, 55, 57, 59, 60*(b)*, 61*(l)*, 63*(r)*, 64*(l and r)*, 65*(all)*, 68*(tl, bl and r)*, 69, 70*(l and r)*, 71*(t and b)*, 73, 80, 81*(all)*, 82, 84*(t and b)*, 85, 86

Keith Glasgow: 20*(t and b)*, 25*(tr)*, 27, 31*(t and br)*, 32, 36–37, 43*(b)*, 47*(bl and br)*, 61*(r)*, 62–63,

Courtesy of the Greek National Tourist Organization: 11

Christine Hilker: 76–77, 78, 79

Jerry Howard/Positive Images: 62*(l)*

Kerr Photography: 9

Christopher Little: 15, 41*(t)*

George Perkin/Cement & Concrete Assoc.: 60*(tr)*

Robert Perron: 30, 51*(bl)*

Tim Street-Porter: 16, 19, 40*(t)*

Shope, Reno, Wharton Associates: 60*(tl)*

Courtesy of U.S.D.A. Soil Conservation Service: 54

KEY TO ILLUSTRATION CODES:
tl: top left; *tr:* top right; *bl:* bottom left; *br:* bottom right;
t: top, *b:* bottom; *l:* left; *r:* right